The Prince of Eejits

(Growing up Irish Catholic before political correctness)

"Lads and Lassies, come here to me now. Life is hard. But it's harder if you're an eejit. Don't be an eejit".

-Father Michael Bueller's advice to the 8th grade graduating class of St. Cecelia's School, Clearwater Florida, 1976.

From the Oxford English Dictionary:

Eejit, noun, informal

Irish and Scottish form of idiot

This memoir is dedicated first to my big brother Brian. I always wanted to be just like you.

And next to my beautiful wife Michelle, who kept encouraging me to write. This would never have been finished without you.

Thanks Bob H. for the edits, and Jimmy who kept telling me, "Man, you got to write this stuff down."

Table of Contents

THE BEGINNING

We moved to Clearwater Florida when I was seven. I was never really quite sure why we ended up in Clearwater. As far as I can remember, I was quite happy living in Illinois. To this day, I really don't know why we left. Along with my Mom and Dad, there was my older brother Brian, two younger sisters Colette and Kathleen, and then Kevin (me).

We lived in a comfortable modest home on Riverside Drive in Libertyville Illinois, a respectable middle class suburb of Chicago. The house had a huge yard to play in, and as a bonus, the Des Plains River ran right behind the house providing endless hours of entertainment for two small boys with big imaginations.

Neither Donald nor Betty Durst had any connection to Florida. My mother was born in a small village outside of Dublin Ireland and my father from what is now an undesirable suburb of North Chicago. Maybe we left because of the Joneses.

Irene and Bernard Jones were our neighbors in that idyllic neighborhood street we lived on in Libertyville. In a neighborhood full of children, I believe they were the only family on the block that did not have kids. Mrs. Jones made up for that though by becoming sort of a surrogate mom to all of us, even babysitting once a week so my parents could go out to the Swedish Glee Club dinners on Tuesday nights.

Maybe it was Mr. Jones' rheumatism or perhaps Mrs. Jones' restlessness that caused them to move to Florida. That was 1966. We followed in 1969, and we stayed with the Jones for a couple of months while my parents looked for a house. My mother immediately joined St. Cecelia's church as parishioners, and then just as quickly enrolled Brian and I at St. Cecelia's Elementary School, my two younger sisters not yet being school age.

Clearwater Florida and The Church

St. Cecilia's Church and school became a microcosm within Clearwater for me. I spent my formative years, and a large part of my adult life in that west coast Florida town. I took only short sabbaticals to attend college, sell books door to door during those college summers and, at a particular point in my life when the Wanderlust burnt bright within, taking off to live in Ireland for a couple years to truly connect with my roots, (and to get down to a serious in depth study of Irish Pub Culture.)

St. Cecelia's was one of the few Catholic churches in West Central Florida in 1969, one of only two I can recall, although more would come. The church was built in 1924 on the corner of Myrtle Ave. and Druid road on a piece of swampland deemed no use for anything but a Catholic church. In this part of the south, Catholics were more often than not referred to as papists, and did not present themselves in any appreciable numbers for fifty years or more after the Civil War.

In 1890, an expedition of Jesuit priests was sent to the area of "Clear Water Harbor" to administer to any Catholics present. An inquisition by the leader of the expedition as to the number of Catholics in the area was met with the reply, "none". Before the erection of the church, Mass was said in private homes, or if one wanted a church, they had to drive to Tampa to attend Sacred Heart, the only Catholic Church in the area at that time.

Even in 1969, this area of Florida was considered wild and wooly heathen country as far as the

Vatican was concerned. My mother, being from Ireland, a country that was 99.9% Roman Catholic, found herself in what her mind was hostile territory. She had heard terrifying stories about the natives, a tribe called Baptists, that would not take a drink (and thus could not be trusted) and would shove your head under water during one of their rituals to force you to convert to their heresy. Not to be intimidated by the heathens all around, Mom immediately started to seek out allies in the sea of Protestantism in which she found herself engulfed.

Those allies she found through the church. The church, and even more so the school, became the central focus for my childhood. My mother was friends with all the Irish parents, and we were friends with all the Irish kids. We celebrated holidays and special events together and the Irish had a lot of pull in the politics of the parish. We all went to school at St. Cecelia's, attended summer camp at Mary Help of Christians, and honestly, I didn't realize there was a religion other than Catholicism until I was in about the eighth grade.

Through the church and the school I formed a tight knit group of friends, many of which I am still in touch with some forty years on. Clearwater was back then still a sleepy backwater town, a sparkling jewel in what would later become known as the Suncoast. Her beaches were still yet undiscovered by the masses. The fishing was on par with today's world class Sportsman's destinations, and best of all, we were allowed to roam her streets on our bikes, day or night, fish the waters and camp the nearby woods and bay islands largely unmolested by rules, regulations or paranoid overprotective parents. In truth we largely ran feral, especially during the summer months. I can imagine that on the rare occasion that a tourist might have spotted us camping on one of the bay islands, or walking through some of the creeks and storm sewers in town, armed with broken off shovels and rakes as spears, they may have thought that they had accidently stumbled on a movie set filming a remake of Lord of the Flies. It was truly an ideal place to be a kid. Or more precisely, an ideal place to be a boy.

The Parish grew quickly and word must have got out in Boston or New York that Clearwater was the place to be for Paddy. Every week there was a new O' Something family showing up at the house, coming in for tea and we were expected to entertain the kids outside while the dads talked sports and the women talked children inside.

The number of priests at St. Cecelia's grew too. Most were Irish and because of the low number of Catholics in Florida, the Vatican had designated the state as Mission Country and targeted as an area for building the faith. Upon joining the missions in their home country, many Irish priests were pleasantly surprised to find themselves, not in equatorial Africa, but in sunny Florida with air conditioning, TVs, modern cars, and in truth, enjoying a higher standard of living than in their native land.

One of those priests was Father Bueller (hereafter also referred to as FB). He was a native of County Clare Ireland and become a central figure in the group of families that made up mine and my parent's friends. My mom became friends with Father Bueller because of a shared heritage. My dad and Father Bueller became friends because of a shared passion, drinking.

Father Bueller the man

Although my father was a committed Catholic, I would not put him in the zealot category, which is where I would firmly place my mother. And although he did love my mother, I don't think he was overly fond of the Irish as a whole if truth be known. He did have some Irish roots. His mother's maiden name was O'Rourke and I do remember some talk between him and my aunt about some of their uncles being involved with the Irish Mob in Chicago. One of my great uncles I do know left Hamburg Germany rather suddenly as a result of the local police there asking a few too many questions about a local murder. And if recollection serves, I believe he did end up working with one of the Northside Irish gangs and ending up in jail, so maybe Dad had it out for the Irish because of that.

Nonetheless, he liked Bueller, he liked drinking with Bueller and it was probably handy for a catholic to have a priest for a drinking buddy. Let's face it. There are always "complications" when drinking moves beyond the social and into the territory of the obsessive. The law comes to mind, and Bueller was nothing if not great at using the collar to explain away to the authorities any legal dilemmas that may present themselves.

In the days before MADD (Mothers Against Drunk Driving), I can remember several occasions when the police would show up at our doorstep with my dad and Father Bueller in tow. They would have been stopped for drunk driving and one of the cops (and yes, a lot of them were Irish) would show up to present the two offenders to my mother. "Hi Betty. Try and keep an eye on these two would you? The car is on the corner of Nursery and Clearwater-Largo Rd. Make sure to pick it up before noon or the tow truck will take it to impound." And as for dilemmas of the moral type and transgressions of the Faith, Bueller, by waving his hand if front of you in the shape of a cross, mumbling something under his breath, and issuing a penance, could absolve you of a variety of sins that always seem to accompany undisciplined drinking. Quite handy really.

Father Bueller also became a central character in my life. Although we had a lot of interactions with clergy between school and church, Father Bueller was special. He was at our house all the time, and despite all his flaws, he was a very funny character with an infectious laugh and childlike enthusiasm. He had striking good looks with jet black hair and piercing, dark eyes. He was well built with chiseled arms, a muscular chest and flat abs. It was easy to believe he had been raised on a farm. Except for his chosen profession, he would have done very well with the ladies.   He was kind to me.

He was close when all other priests were distant. He makes me laugh every time I think about him today. I can see him now, huge smile, sparkling eyes, and after telling a funny story, laughing heartily and fiercely rubbing his hands together until I thought they would burst into flames. I loved Father Bueller and I miss him. Most of all, Father Bueller was a character.   He was a great character.

In an age today where we are bombarded by messages of political correctness, what we should do, how we should do it, who needs to accept us, who we need to get approval from, we forget the importance of individuality and where individuality comes from, the individual.   He was who he was and cared not what you thought. He knew he was flawed and accepted it. He knew you were flawed and accepted you. He forgave himself and he forgave others, (not a bad character trait for a priest). He touched many of the people around him and left lifelong impressions on those he knew, as this childhood reminiscence will attest.

Bueller was the seventh son in a large Irish farming family. Whether he was the seventh son of a seventh son I do not know. I somehow doubt it, as the healing powers ascribed to such a man, outside of the ability to cure a hangover, (which I more readily believe came from much trial and error through a journey of personal discovery), appear to have eluded the good father.

Some say that the younger sons in an Irish farming family generally ended up with the short end of any stick that might be had. I cannot say for sure if that was the case with Father Bueller. While I'm sure that the eldest boy got the farm, as was the custom, that does not mean that there was nothing left for the younger siblings. The popular story, whether it is to stir up sympathy for the younger sons or simply an attempt to explain the proliferation of Irish priests, was that the younger sons had no choice but to go into the priesthood if they wanted an education or any kind of life. Regardless of the series of events that led to his taking of vows, Bueller was in the priesthood. Although Father Bueller made a great priest, at least in my opinion, he was probably not classic priest material. I kind of think that Bueller may not have gone into the priesthood completely voluntarily or with a great enthusiasm or a rush of euphoria as the result of an overwhelming calling by the Almighty. The saying that God works through cracked pots, certainly applies to Father Bueller.

Although he took his vows seriously and really wanted to serve the Lord, he was not entirely happy with being a priest and there were signs.

There was the alcohol abuse. Of course compulsive overconsumption is not the exclusive domain of Irish priests. However, they do seem to have a particular knack for it and tend to pull it off with a certain amount of style what with the singing, storytelling carrying on and such.

There was the drug abuse. Quaaludes, known as Soapers, were a favorite.

Methaqualone, or Quaaludes, or ludes, were a very popular sedative hypnotic drug in the late 60's and early 70's. It was the sixth best-selling sedative in the legal US market and quickly shot to number one in the recreational category. They became known as *"disco biscuits"* to those who enjoyed popping them and then dancing all night at glam rock clubs. And on college campuses across America, *"luding out"* (taking qualudes and washing them down with alcohol, passing out and then having a complete blackout concerning the previous twenty four hours) was all the rage.

I'm not completely sure how Father Bueller originally got involved with Soapers. Whether it was innocently enough through a prescription for an injury, an operation, or difficulty sleeping, or he actively sought them out, I do not know. Regardless, once the two of them were introduced, it was love at first sight. Like a passionate love story, when they were together it burned wildly, sometimes out of control, apart, and they painfully pined for each other.

Now I do have to comment here briefly on the good Father's use of prescription narcotics. In an era today where nearly half of the adult population is on some sort of pain killer or antidepressant, regular consumption of strong psychoactive drugs may seem benign. However, in the early '70s, it was still considered somewhat irregular. Believe it or not, being diagnosed with a psychotic condition and put on medication was not worn as the Badge of Honor that it is today. As a matter of fact, and I know this sounds weird, but people actually went to great lengths to hide their mental conditions and their addictions.

Hidden or out in the open, the problem of securing a steady supply still presented itself. You see, when you start using these things on a regular basis, you need a pretty good supply to sustain daily use and to mitigate the inevitable tolerance one builds up to any drug used on a continuous basis. To the uninitiated, these drugs would have been difficult to find. Oh certainly they could be had illegally, but going into seedy neighborhoods in search of illicit drugs would not have been the Padre's first choice.

However, if it had come to that, Bueller would have pulled it off with style. I can, with complete plausibility, imagine Father Bueller setting up some sort of Catholic Mission in a drug infested neighborhood (with funds he had coerced from the Bishop) and in the process of providing spiritual comfort to the locals, he would have made his connections. Fortunately it didn't come to that.

Pain clinics were not an option. They had not yet become ubiquitous across the fruited plains so you could not just march in to any one of a dozen clinics in your hometown, complain of a backache, and walk out with a six month supply of synthetic heroine as you can today. Certainly your regular physician may prescribe to you once, but more than likely they were not going to give you fifty one refills to cover the rest of the year. The answer? Father Bueller invented Doctor Shopping.

Wearing the priest's collar as his credentials, Bueller would visit multiple physicians complaining of various ailments, real or imaginary, for which he would reluctantly accept a prescription.

I can only imagine the exchange between the pious Irish priest and the old Sawbones. "Well, Father, I can't really find anything physically wrong with you, but you say you're in pain?" "Ahh, Jaysus Doc it's desperate." The good Father would explain. "You should have seen the state of me just this morning. It was only by a true Act of the Almighty that I was able to get out of bed at all and make it down to the homeless shelter for my weekly visit to provide comfort and spiritual guidance for those poor lost souls." "Well", the old Doc would respond, "I suppose I could prescribe some qualudes for you, but I must warn you, they are awfully strong." Father Bueller would strenuously object, "Oh no, no, no, that would be against my principles, no drugs absolutely not. The Lord will give me strength!" The doctor interjects, "But Father you must, you're in pain." "No, no, no, sure didn't our Lord himself suffer on the cross in more pain than I to forgive our sins; this is my cross to bear!" Reluctantly, the Doctor gives in. "We'll, if that's the way you…" Bueller interjects, "Doctor, what exactly do you have in mind?" The Doctor reflects. "Well I guess we could try some low dosage valium. That might provide some relief". Father Bueller thoughtfully considers, "Well, I suppose if we're going to go down that road we might as well do it right. Let's go with the qualudes. I like the brand name not the generics and let's do the 20mg instead of the 10".

18

The result; Father Bueller got his drugs, the physicians felt good about helping a noble soul (priests were still held in high regard back then) and Doctor Shopping was born. His groundbreaking work can be seen today in the proliferation of pain clinics on every corner of major and minor cities and towns across America. In the area of prescription drug abuse, FB really showed incredible individual initiative and imagination. Father Bueller was a true pioneer, a real trail blazer in the field of chronic self-medication

So there was the alcohol use and the drug use, but those are not two activities completely incompatible with the priesthood. However, there is one activity that is, and I specifically remember one incident where it really clicked with me that maybe the priesthood was not Father Bueller's true calling.

We were at what I think was the only restaurant I ever remember going to as a kid. It was called Chief Charley's and its novelty was an all you can eat salad bar, the only one of its kind in Clearwater at that time. My mother loved the place. Even the cheapest meals came with the salad bar and she could fill up two growing boys on endless salad followed by the Salisbury steak platter. On the rare occasions when we did go out to eat, it was always with the Chief. Father Bueller loved the Chief too, but for a different reason, cheap booze.

I think Father Bueller really hated to drink alone, and my brother Brian and I (heretofore after referred to also as "The Lads"), would often go with him. Now many people look down on drinking alone, but the Irish more so than most. If you're going to just sit down at a table with a bottle and pour booze into yourself for the sake of getting drunk, as is common in some cultures that is one thing.

(I had a Polish roommate when I was living in Ireland that actually insisted on drinking alone. A bottle of potato vodka was simply a ticket to a destination and no traveling companion was required or wanted. We actually came home one night after being out drinking and singing with friends at a pub in Dublin to find Rolf passed out on the couch, empty liter bottle of vodka on the floor, as he made his return trip home.

His snoring was unbearable and any attempt to wake him or move him was fruitless. We finally had to pick up the entire couch and put it outside the apartment on the sidewalk. It was a cold night in Dublin, so we piled on several heavy comforters to keep him warm. Coincidently, our neighbor was moving to Wales on the morning ferry the next day and had arranged for a friend to come by in his truck to pick up her furniture and some boxes that were to be left outside and taken to the dock. The movers thought that our couch with Rolf ensconced beneath the covers was just part of the goods to be collected and threw him on the truck with the other stuff. The mistake was actually not discovered until about halfway across the Irish Sea when an angry ferry master, investigating what he thought was a diesel engine left idling, found Rolf in the back of the truck still snoring away. Rolf returned from Holyhead Wales back to Dublin on the next ferry and so there'd be no hard feelings we wired him the money for the return ticket. We felt it was the right thing to do, but I digress)

As for the Irish, if you're going to drink, you're going to sing. And if you're going to sing, you're going to play music and if you're going to play music, you're going to tell stories so you better have a couple of friends with you to do it right.

Now I'm not saying that Father Bueller didn't have friends to drink with. God knows my mother went out on many a night to pick up FB when he and some friends had had a few too many. Well, let's just be honest here. For them to have called my mother, they would have been out of their bleeding minds drunk, had either lost the keys, lost the car, lost the keys and the car, or nobody could see

,even with one eye covered up, well enough to drive. That phone call to my mother would have been an absolute last resort. Over the years, she had picked up assorted collections of priests, Knights of Columbus members and any number of St. Cecelia parishioners that may have been out with the good father for the evening. So I know he had friends.

I think he took my brother and me with him when he wanted to drink privately but not alone. It was often in a restaurant and when it wasn't he was at our house drinking. We would have been fourteen, fifteen and 16 years old and certainly we did not have the identification or the appearance to be allowed to drink in a bar, especially in a time when the age of consent was twenty one.

The good father had no problem ordering drinks for us (beer only, no hard liquor ,the man was a responsible member of the Catholic Clergy after all) When questioned by the waitress about our age, Father Bueller would step in to quickly vouch for us, throw in some nonsense about us being on our way to a pilgrimage, a religious retreat, going off to help blind deaf children in equatorial Guyana or some such thing as that, and that he was in charge, he would take full responsibility, etc., etc., etc. We almost never failed to get served. Despite the few beers he allowed us to drink, I believe deep down he had a real *en loco parentis* sense of responsibility toward us. He wanted the best for us and I believe in some way he wanted to be a part of our lives to make up for the fact that my Dad had passed away and was no longer around. Besides, if he ended up getting too hammered, he would need one of us to drive him back to the rectory.

And here may be Father Bueller's first big contribution to my education. I actually learned how to drive a stick shift well before I had a license to drive any vehicle as a result of occasionally having to take the helm of a '69 VW Bug (borrowed from a parishioner) that Bueller was driving as a result of having his primary conveyance, a 1970 sky blue Chevy Nova, impounded by the Bishop in a futile attempt by His Excellency to keep the good Father's drinking confined to the grounds of the church. Opportunities to expand your horizons and learn are always there if you're just willing to look for them.

So that's where we were, in the Chief Charley lounge, when it really hit me that the priesthood was probably not where Father Bueller needed to be. We were seated in a booth, my brother Brian, myself, the good Father and on stage a three piece ensemble wearing velvet leisure suits was cajoling us every third song or so to try the veal and that they would be there all week. I kind of think if that

23

place hadn't been bulldozed twenty years ago that band would still be there. Yes, that's where it first struck me that maybe the priesthood wasn't Michael Bueller's calling at all. You see it was the cocktail waitresses.

They wore impossibly short skirts, almost Playboy bunny with short frilly lace in place of the tail, black stockings and high heels. It was a very disturbing outfit for a fourteen year old boy, but even more so for Father Bueller. He could not keep his eyes off of them and with each passing drink they were becoming more and more of a distraction. He would periodically go into a short Al Pacino style "Scent of a Woman" rant about the attributes of the fairer sex, and after about the fifth or sixth Jack and ginger, he would offer up little tidbits of advice making me wonder later if maybe there had been a few broken hearts suffered prior to his vows.

"Find yourself good women lads!!" he would say as he pointed a shaky index finger across the table at us. "But Kevin, don't fall in with the harpies, the harpies are everywhere! Promise me you'll stay clear of the harpies". I would promise FB absolutely, "No Harpies", having at the time no idea what a harpy was.

The harpies admonition was a pretty good indicator that now would be a good time to start trying to get the keys to the Bug, as I would probably be taking the tiller on the way back to the Rectory. Sometimes I felt sad for Father Bueller, and you could tell that at times, his vow of celibacy weighed heavy on him. It was his cross to bear.

Father Bueller the Priest

At the same time Father Bueller was a good priest and performed his duties well, sometimes a little too well. As an altar boy I was able to see all the comings and goings behind the scenes at St. Cecelia's Church. Each priest had his own reputation. Father Bueller had the reputation of being the priest you wanted to see on the altar if you were in a hurry. Many of the other priests could never figure out why Father Bueller's Sunday service was so popular. I knew, and so did many of the hundreds that would pack his mass.

He wasn't a great speaker. He rattled off a sermon in a high speed monotone that, combined with his West Ireland accent, often made it almost totally undecipherable. He was not a particularly gifted theologian. There were several other priests with much more impressive resumes. No, what Father Bueller brought to the table was sheer speed. A typical Catholic service takes about forty-five minutes to an hour depending on the number for communion and the length of the homily. Now I've seen some priests get through a mass fairly lively, but nothing like Bueller. I've witnessed FB say Mass, from procession in the door to procession out, in twenty three minutes flat. If you were in a hurry, Bueller was your man. Although I never saw it, I like to think that someday Father Bueller may have broken the twenty minute mass.

Of course going to a Father Bueller service was also something of a crap shoot. Just because he was scheduled to say High Mass and his name appeared next to the Mass in the weekly bulletin, didn't always mean he would actually show up. Father Bueller approached the Mass schedule with much the same attitude that many men approach a "honey do" list. It's definitely something we plan to do, we promise, we're kind of committed, but if a better deal comes up, all bets are off. In the case that FB got a better offer, the church goer planning on a Father Bueller Mass and being back home in time for the Sunday game, may end up with a Father Burghdorf Mass in which case there was a good chance you could be there until Monday morning. Yes, a Father Bueller Mass had its rewards, but like anything, there were risks.

Unfortunately, the good father's cavalier attitude toward services did not end with just the one sacrament. Weddings and funerals could be a bit dodgy as well. A no show at a funeral wasn't too serious, as the guest of honor probably did not have elaborate plans post ceremony. Weddings were another thing. I can remember several calls that came to our house from Monsignor Harkin asking if we had seen or knew the whereabouts of

FB, as there was a an anxious couple, guests, and limos arriving at St. Cecelia's church and apparently they were there expecting a wedding.

Although this was certainly not a common occurrence, I know it happened more than once, but it was always a sore point. It was bad enough when a man or a woman was left at the altar by a fiancé with cold feet, but very rarely did you ever hear about a *couple* being left at the altar. Fortunately, not too much damage was ever done. For the most part, there was always another priest readily available to step in and send the hopeful couple happily on their way to wedded bliss. (Apparently, at the rectory, the other priests had organized themselves that whenever Bueller was scheduled to do a wedding, they rearranged their schedules to be available just to give the good father some "bench strength".) However, there was a rumor, and I repeat, this was only a rumor, that one jilted couple got into such a fierce fight over being left at the altar by Bueller that they decided not to get married at all. It's my understanding that when the Vatican figured Bueller's lifetime statistics as a priest, number of masses said, number of baptisms, funerals, weddings, etc., that in all fairness, they subtracted "wedding no shows" from "weddings performed" to arrive at a "net" figure for the marriage category.

The one sacrament he took very seriously, never rushed and seemed to perform quite regularly was confession. He easily spent at least two hours in the confessional for every hour of his closest competitor.

If you've never been in a confession box, it really is an interesting device. It's basically a small closet with two doors, one for the priest and one for the sinner. There is a wall dividing priest from parishioner and a small sliding opaque door opened (operated by the priest) to connect penance giver to penitent. You couldn't really see the priest, just sort of a shadow, but you could of course hear him and he could hear you. Although I believe the idea was for both parties to remain anonymous, in the tightly woven community of St. Cecelia's, you knew the priest by his voice and he knew you by yours, but everybody played along that nobody knew who was who.

Confession is actually an amazing ritual if you think about it. I can think of no other institution in society where one can, in fifteen minutes, be completely cleansed, potentially, of a lifetime of wrongdoing by simply kneeling in a small box, declaring your transgressions, saying you're sorry and saying a few prayers. Anguish and apprehensions that would take years and tens of thousands of dollars to sort out with a high priced shrink or therapist can simply be handed over to the man in the box and in return you are granted absolution.   One can unload a lifetime of grief and regrets, poor choices and poor virtue, public trespass and private turpitude, free of charge, and the person swapping the peccadillos for pardon is sworn by sacred vow and protected by law from ever revealing them here on earth.

As kids, we viewed Confession as the ultimate "Get out of Jail Free Card".

But it was also a place where, especially if Father Bueller was the priest in the box, you might be able to get a few answers on some things.

Sex is a very confusing thing for a pubescent boy in the Catholic Church. We heard constantly about the Virgin Mary, but were never told what that meant. I thought for a time that "Virgin" was her first name and "Mary" her last, or that maybe Virgin was her name before she married Joseph, but that didn't make sense because when our teacher, Miss Fragola became Mrs. Stuart, it was her last name that changed not her first and I didn't know what Joseph's last name was, but I was sure it wasn't either Virgin or Mary, so that didn't figure.

Once, while deep in thought about this issue, I blurted out at lunch to Miss Harris, who unbeknownst to me at the time was gaining a reputation among the faculty for promiscuity, "What's a Virgin?" I was given a clip across the ear and threatened with a trip to the office.

The only time I ever heard about sex from my parents was during a game of Scrabble. My mother laid down an "S" next to two letters to form The Word. My heart stopped, and so did I. "It's your turn, my Mom said" It took all the courage I could muster to ask, "What's that?", pointing at "The Word". I readied myself. I felt weak all over. My heart was pounding. This is it. I was going to find out, the mystery would be revealed. "Sex?", my Mom said. "That's whether you are a boy or a girl. My sex is a girl, your sex is you're a boy. Go ahead and roll."

That was it. That was all I got. Oh sure, there was plenty of talk among us boys, but most of it sounded crazy, even from Roger Murphy who had two older sisters and professed to be an expert at such things. But quite frankly, some of the things he talked about seemed completely implausible. Nobody did those kinds of things to each other, certainly not my mother!

My mom did later give me a book. "A Catholic Boy's Guide to his Body". It was written by a priest with the forward written by a nun. Talk about the uninitiated leading the ignorant. There weren't even any dirty pictures in it.

She didn't sit down with me and explain why she was giving me the book, what I would learn, or tell me anything about what was in the book. One morning while rushing to get to school in time, she simply showed me the book and said, "Here's a book for you. If you have any questions, ask Father Bueller", and shoved the book in my book bag and headed me off for school.

Well, that's exactly what I did.

At St. Cecelia's School, Mass every Friday in the school cafeteria was mandatory. A priest would come from St. Cecelia's church to say the mass and once a month, he would stay and hear confession. Once a month confession was also mandatory for the older students. It seemed that Father Bueller was the priest more often than not on those Confession Fridays, so I got to spend a lot of time with FB in the confession box.

When a priest other than Bueller was in the box, we often made up a litany of sins which I'm sure we were guilty of anyway, confessed them to the priest, got our penance and we were happily on our way. All was forgiven, the slate cleaned and ready to be soiled again. With Father Bueller, most of us guys liked to go to him because we could talk more openly with him, and it seemed like he cared and wanted to know not just what the sin was but

how we felt about it.   Father Bueller dug deep
going beyond the sin to get to motivation. A
typical exchange for us adolescent boys would go
something like this:

"Bless me Father for I have sinned. It has been
one month since my last confession" Father
Bueller would respond, "Confess your sins to
Almighty God my Son." At that point, we would
usually rattle of the usual list of standard sins that
you were sort of required to confess: I lied, I stole
something, I cheated on a test, I said a couple of
swear words and then we would generally ease
into what was really on our minds. "Ugh, father,
I've also had some thoughts."   "Thoughts my
Son?" "Ugh, yea Father it's just that, ugh, well,
Jaysus, Father it's Mary O'Connell. I can't take my
eyes off of her; I mean, have you seen the chassis
on that Lassie? Augh, the things I want to do to
her Father. I've had some terrible thoughts father,
awful, disgusting, sinful, repugnant thoughts."
......"Go on my son." ...." Well, that's just it Father,
it's thoughts, horrible, disgusting, vile thoughts. I
think about it all the time. I want to touch her,
ugh, you know, I want to feel her, mmm, well you
know, her parts, father, her things, her bits and
pieces, oh Jaysus father it's dreadful, am I damned
to Hell?"   "Not at all Son." The good father
would press on.   "Now is it just Mary O'Connell
or are there others?...."Oh God no Father, it's not
just Mary. It's Sandra Martinez and Julie Bane and

Kathleen O'Conner and Juliet, oh good Lord Father, Juliet Wheeler........" FB would intervene, "Yes, yes son. I understand. It's hard." Of course that was the problem, it was hard all the time. It was hard when I woke up, it was hard in class, it was hard in the lunchroom, and good Lord, when I got around Mary McConnell, was it ever hard.

Bueller was never fazed. "Yes, yes my son, I understand." Now of course for a Catholic, certainly pre-marital sex was a sin, but just the very thoughts a normal adolescent boy had about every thirty eight seconds or so were also sinful. We were terrified that a priest might think that we were some kind of horrible deviants because of such thoughts, but FB set our minds to ease assuring us that these thoughts were completely normal and nothing to be ashamed of. Even the sin of masturbation, or "choking the Bishop", as it was known to us young Catholic adolescents, was certainly something to be avoided, but not something that was going to condemn our young souls to eternal damnation.

When FB made sure you had it all off your chest, he assigned you a couple of Hail Mary's, a few Our Fathers, a Glory be to God or two and you were forgiven. Brilliant! A true miracle. Father Bueller let you know that it was okay to be human, it was ok with God and you felt better about yourself after having spent a little time with FB "in the box". Yes, I think that's where Father Bueller really shined. Some priests give great Mass, others do a bang up Baptism, but no one came near Father Bueller when it came to a corker of a confession.

So I guess between Chief Charley's, the VW Bug, and the confessional at school, Father Bueller taught me about cars and women, two things every young man needs a guide to. Knowledge of both would be essential several years later when I became a man in the back seat of a 1970 Buick Skylark at Crest Lake Park.

St. Cecelia the Church

As I mentioned, most of my early life revolved around St. Cecelia's Church, School and the various functions associated with each. My mother worked for the Church, or more precisely for the Diocese of St. Petersburg in the marriage tribunal. My brother and I were Altar Boys, serving at least one Mass each Sunday, and both of us, along with my two sisters, attended St. Cecelia's School.

My mother's office, the Marriage Tribunal, was the agency where Catholics who were divorced could come and petition the Church to be remarried in the Catholic faith. But before they could remarry, the first marriage had to be nullified. This was called an annulment of the marriage, in essence, the Catholic Church declaring that in the eyes of God, the marriage never existed.

Now I always found this fascinating. I mean, here was a couple who had been married in the Catholic Church, at the altar in front of God and in a ceremony performed by a priest and witnessed perhaps by hundreds of their friends and family. They pledged, "…for better or for worse…so help me God…and I Dos". There were wedding photos and dresses, houses bought together, taxes paid jointly, her name legally changed, children and perhaps even grandchildren. Yet, with the filing of some paperwork and a few affidavits, The Church would declare, not that they were getting a pass and could have a "do-over", or even that they were forgiven of the sin of divorce, and could try again, but that the whole thing *never happened!*

It kind of reminds you of the old Soviet Union or Maoist China where they "disappeared" people. You'd work thirty years at the People's Underwear and Sock Company Number 124 and then come in one day and ask about the guy in the cubicle next to you who had been there for twenty nine of those thirty years, "Hey, where's Bob?" The guy two cubicles down would answer, "Bob?, Bob who?"…"You know, Bob, the guy who has been sitting next to us here for twenty nine years, Bob?" Again, with no eye contact and a monotone voice the reply would come, "That cubicle has always been empty and I don't know anyone named Bob."

And the bar was set pretty low in order for the Church to disappear a marriage. The inability to have children was cause, as was domestic violence, homosexuality and drug abuse. Okay, fair enough. But also included as cause was alcoholism, which meant that myself, eighty percent of my friends and the entire country of Ireland were in danger at any moment of becoming bastard children.

Unfortunately my mother brought her work home with her, and I came home from school almost daily to hear stories of horrific marriages that had broken up, the physical abuse, betrayal, deceit, financial destruction and ruined lives as a result of this thing called marriage. I grew up with this perverted view that marriage was some sort of institutionalized hell, (and yes, I know, there are some out there that would argue that my original conclusion was correct, however, after being married fifteen years now and having enjoyed thirteen years of happy marriage, I would not count myself among their number). I grew up with a strong conviction that marriage was something to be avoided at all costs. It really is a miracle I got married at all. Although I did take the plunge, I was the last of my siblings to do so having managed to avoid blissful union until I was nearly forty.

St. Cecelia the School

The school was run by a particularly strict order of
nuns whose convent ,or "the Hive" as we called it,
was located just off school property on the
opposite bank of a creek that ran along the western
edge of the school grounds.
My childhood friends and I constantly theorized
about what took place after school hours in that
stately white two story house across that slow
moving stream.   You see, we only ever saw the
nuns during the day and always wearing their
dazzlingly white cardboard starched habits with
full head gear. As a matter of fact, to this day, I
have no idea what color hair any of the good
sisters had. This alone become an area of intense
speculation amongst us boys.

Roger Murphy insisted that all the nuns were bald,
and the reason they became nuns was to hide their
baldness. This seemed a little farfetched as I had
never seen or heard of a bald woman. "Exactly!"
Roger said. "That's because they all became
nuns". The logic did seem inescapable, and in
matters concerning girls or women, we gave
Roger's opinion a little extra weight because, after
all, he did have those two older sisters. We
speculated about those nuns all our years. A plan
to sneak up to the window of the convent at night
and peek in fizzled out as a game of "rock, paper,
scissors" to pick the Peeping Tom went into

perpetuity as the loser kept insisting on " one more try". Even a pool that got up to twelve dollars to yank the habit off Sister Mary Wintergreen's head went unclaimed as the nuns' reputation for ferocity became their best defense.

Brian (far left) with some of his "Posse"

Those childhood friends were a tight knit group of catholic boys whose lives were just as closely intertwined with the day to day coming and goings of the church as my own. The core group was Jeff Irwin whose father was a local chef and cooked all the meals at the Irwin home, something we found strange and somewhat suspicious as we knew of no other father who ever cooked anything for anybody. Ron Grimes was being raised by a single Mom, (an anomaly back then), who we irreverently referred to as "yellow" for the way she pronounced "hello" when she answered the phone. Mike and Guy Keenan whose father was a contractor and mother was an international tennis champ. Various others would come and go as part of our group, the Pittmans, Voilands, O'Conners, Mahoney's, et al.

Each day we faced the nuns at St. Cecelia's. Father Bueller's gentler, kinder approach was in marked contrast to that taken by the Sisters of the Holy Cross who were in charge of the day to day proceedings at St. Cecelia's Elementary. As young students, we were constantly assured that the Sisters were "firm, but fair". We became convinced that the sisters were firm but fairly sadistic.

Now I have heard over the years, while exchanging war stories with other survivors of Catholic schools, a multitude of stories surrounding various forms of physical discipline, not the least famous of which is the smashing of the hands and knuckles with the dreaded pointer. The pointer in these recounted tales of childhood

cruelty ranges in size from a handy pocket version
that miraculously appears from beneath a formless
black habit to strike suddenly at an unsuspecting
child's hand during a momentary lapse in good
behavior, to a yardstick size model carried in open
view at all times and whose wrath is announced in
advance, the victim of which is then expected to
present the offending appendages in anticipation of
the blows.

I have to say here that in nine years of Catholic
schooling, I never received, nor was I witness to,
the dreaded knuckle beating. Not to say that this
did not happen at St. Cecelia's, it's just that I never
saw it or heard of it. I say this with some
apprehension as saying that in nine years of
Catholic schooling you were never "knuckled" nor
did you ever witness a "knuckling" will have some
Catholic school survivors doubting whether you
ever attended Catholic school at all. It's something
akin to being a holocaust denier and living in a
Jewish community.

Now I'm not saying that there wasn't physical
discipline that bordered on abuse. Of course there
was. This was after all Catholic school in the old
days. Maybe our nuns at St. Cecelia's didn't
engage in physical abuse because, by a happy
stroke of fate, or perhaps it was planned, they had
a more than competent proxy.

His name was Colonel Good. He was US Army retired and a combat veteran of both World War II and Korea (and five time winner of the World's most Ironic Name Contest). They say that during the war, he was held captive by the Red Chinese, but even the communists released him after three days because they couldn't stand having the miserable son of a bitch around. He returned to combat but was forced to retire because of an almost one hundred percent hearing loss, the result of a mortar round hitting too close to his position. There were allegations that it was friendly fire from his own troops, but nothing could be proven. Twenty years later his next duty station was Boys PE Instructor at St. Cecelia's Elementary School in Clearwater Florida.

Colonel Good was "Old School", that is, medieval Dark Ages type old school. I had him every day for three years, from third grade to fifth. I still remember the drill every PE class. We had no locker rooms so us boys would take our gym clothes into the lavatory and change there, and then run down to the outdoor basketball courts. Once there, we had to line up around the perimeter of the court in alphabetical order. The Colonel would then call us to attention, where we had to stick out our right arm, assuring an arm's length between each boy and then come to a stiff military attention. He would then inspect his troops.

We were terrified every day. Woe be it to the boy with the untied shoe or the dirty gym shirt. But the worst offense was to be out of alphabetical order.

GOOD: "Durst! what are you doing standing next to Stevens?". DURST: (no response, frozen with terror but a gathering moistness forming in the crotch of my gym shorts). GOOD: "Does Durst start with an "s"? Does Durst start with a "t"? Does Durst start with an "r"? DURST :(still just panicked silence). GOOD: "what letter of the alphabet does Durst start with son? Do you know your alphabet son? DURST: "yes sir" GOOD:" I can't hear you". DURST: "YES SIR!". Good: "I STILL can't hear you!" (now remember, this guy is almost 100% deaf, he really can't hear me). DURST: "YES SIR!!!" GOOD: "Okay Durst, if you're not going to talk, let's see how you walk. Give me ten laps on the girl's court."

There were two concrete basketball courts on that old schoolyard. One was called the boy's court and the other the girl's court. There was no physical difference between the courts, just that one was used for calisthenics, basketball, volleyball and other sports. The other court was Colonel Good's personal torture chamber.

The Colonel employed two basic forms of punishment, both I'm convinced he learned from the Red Chinese. There was the duck walk and the

44

crab walk. The duck walk had the victim assume a squatting position and then tuck each thumb under his armpits, walking in the squatted position, flapping your arms and quacking periodically, up and down the basketball court for the required number of laps. The crab walk had the victim starting by laying on his back and then lifting himself up with his arms and legs and then walking backward in that position for as many laps as the offense had dictated. This was a much more difficult way to walk, but at least you retained some dignity as you were not required to make crab noises as you walked down the court. All this was carried out on scorching hot concrete, ninety five degree heat and ninety percent humidity. Eventually the crab walk was dropped from the repertoire when Andrew O'Conner split his wrist and passed out from heat exhaustion on lap thirty when Good forgot to tell him how many laps to do and O'Conner, out of fear, just kept going until he collapsed.

Colonel Good was also a big fan of encouraging us boys to settle our differences like men. He loved when the occasional schoolyard scrap erupted between classmates. A fight was a big event, and even with his impaired hearing, Colonel Good could always detect when one was about to break out. At the first signs of potential pugilists, a sparkle could be seen in the Colonel's eye and then slowly a smile would creep across his face as he surveyed the landscape to determine where the skirmish may be happening. All activities were put on hold for the event, as all boys were required to drop what they were doing and head for the scene of the engagement.

When not enough scraps broke out naturally between ten, eleven and twelve year old boys, Good would pick a fight for us. You never knew when it might happen. Sometimes, just out of the blue, the Colonel would pick out his contestants. "Hey Durst, Quinn here says your sister smells like pig vomit. What do you think about that?" Quinn would be standing behind the Colonel with a terrified look on his face shaking his head back and forth and waving his hands knowing what was coming next. "So what are you going to do about it Durst, let him get away with that?" "Get over here and defend your sister's honor"

When a fight did break out, Good was the first one there. He would blow his whistle loudly and constantly, but not to try and break up the fight. The whistle blowing was a notice to the rest of us to surround the participants so the nuns couldn't see what was going on. As the crowd of boys gathered to cloak the fight, jeers, shouts and insults were directed toward the fighters. "Hey you pansies, you look like you're kissing, hit the guy!" and "I've seen better fights during girls PE" "Don't let him grab your goodies" Every once in a while even one of us boys made a comment, but our jobs were mainly to watch out for the nuns and tell Good if they were approaching. Eventually Good would break it up, or they would tire, and the participants would be forced into a half- hearted handshake and then sent to the lavatory to clean up.

Good ended up losing his position at St. Cecelia's as a result of the fights. It wasn't actually the fights per se that caused Good's dismissal, but they provided the vehicle to reveal a certain character flaw that the nuns simply couldn't tolerate. As it turned out, the colonel was something of an anti-Semite. It started when he picked a fight for David Stein with a much bigger, older and stronger boy. Good then started in with the comments. "Come on you little kike bastard defend yourself", and "come on Stein put up a fight. Pretend he owes you a nickel." But as the fight broke up he said "you need a tattoo like your mother Stein. Maybe I should tattoo "loser" on your forearm." And as he turned around he was face to face with Sister Regina Reilly who had witnessed the whole thing. Good was out and Bob Marley (not the reggae rocker) took his place. Marley was nonmilitary but cut from the same cloth with the same "the beatings will continue until student morale improves" attitude.

So Colonel Good, and then Marley pretty much took care of any physical abuse that was deemed necessary at St. Cecelia's, but that's not to say that the good sisters didn't carry their weight when it came to dishing out the emotional and mental abuse.

My personal tormentor was Sister Mary Wintergreen. For some reason I became her favorite target for ridicule and the more she called me out the more I pushed back, and it simply escalated from there.

It started off with pretty benign stuff. I would offend her by talking in class and I would have to go stand in the corner for the rest of the period. Now I mean the corner. My feet would have to be touching the walls and my face literally inches from the wall for a half hour to forty five minutes. I think if she could have gotten her hands on a dunce cap, she would have made me wear it. But at least this was still passive humiliation.

It escalated though. This woman just really hated people talking in her class and I guess she took it as a personal offense that someone would speak while she was trying to impart her great body of knowledge into our young empty skulls. One day I was invited to explain to the class why what I had to say was so much more important than what she was saying.

SISTER MARY WINTERGREEN (SMW): "Mr. Durst, I see you are engaged in another of your intellectual dialogues with Mr. Murphy back there. I'm sure what you're talking about is much more important, much more enlightening than this silly little discussion I'm having about ancient Athens and the beginnings of all of Western Civilization. Please pray tell, what is the topic of your intellectual discourse with Mr. Murphy? No, please tell me NOW! Oh, yo yos. You're discussing yo yos. Please come up front here so we can all learn more about yo yos. This little discussion about the birth of Western Civilization can surely wait such a pressing and heady matter as yo yos. Please come up front before the class. Class don't you all want to hear from Mr. Durst? Of course you do."

So I would come up before the class. SMW: "Class, this is a member of the Intelligencia. The Intelligencia is an elite group of individuals who feel that their opinions and what they have to say is much more important than anything the rest of us may want to discuss. How do I know this? Well it's obvious. I have a degree from Columbia University and a PhD from Notre Dame University, yet Mr. Durst still feels he must share his vast knowledge of yo-yos with Mr. Murphy while I'm discussing the rise of Western Civilization. Tell me Mr. Durst, where did you get your PhD in yo-yos. Oh come Mr. Durst, a moment ago you had so much to say to Mr. Murphy on the subject. Please enlighten the rest of us. Maybe you'd like to tell the class about the rise of the Athenian Greek City State? No? How about sharing with us your vast knowledge of Greek Philosophy? Perhaps some brief commentary on the teachings of Plato? No, nothing? Class this is someone going nowhere in life. When you are grown and going through the pickup window at McDonald's, this is the face that will be staring back at you. Mr. Durst take your seat." Lunch followed SMW's class, and did I look forward to hearing that bell.

Is it Lunch Yet?

I loved Lunch. It wasn't necessarily because I was starving, although I was. Breakfast everyday consisted of two scrambled eggs and one slice of toast at seven am and by noon I was famished. But I was always hungry as a kid. My Mom did her best, but it was tough to keep four kids, especially two big growing boys, fed, clothed and sheltered on a church secretary's salary.

I'm not saying we didn't have plenty to eat. We had plenty. Every time I asked my mom for more to eat she would say, "No, you've had plenty", so I know we had plenty. I was always looking forward to the next meal and that meal was always just enough to keep me going, but always focused on the meal to come. The most strictly enforced rules during my childhood didn't revolve around school, or homework or chores, but rather, food.

We had the most amazing milk jug in our refrigerator. Mom would buy milk by the gallon, first in glass containers and later in plastic, and then mark the halfway point on the jug with a black marker. We were not allowed to drink past this point. Miraculously, every other evening or so, the jug would regenerate itself going from half full or less-(mom was allowed to consume below "the mark") to full overnight. We never questioned this. We were just delighted to see that the milk was north of the mark giving us the green light to drink. We found out later that my mom would get powdered milk that was donated to the church and add that to the regular milk so it would go twice as far.

My mom had every meal planned out and every scrap of leftovers from those dinners were figured into a future meal. Woe be it to the child who snuck into the fridge at night to soothe a growling tummy or grabbed a snack after school and jeopardized a future meal. The only time I ever remember seeing my mom cry, other than when my father died, involved food.

It was a Sunday, and after church my mother was preparing a special meal. I don't remember it being a holiday, although it might have been. Or it may have been one of our birthdays, I can't remember, but it was a big deal. My mother was cooking a roast beef. This was huge, and on those rare occasions that a Roast beef or a leg of lamb graced the Durst table, mom was extraordinarily proud. A tablecloth was laid upon the table, the good dishes brought out and the food was placed in bowls and plates and laid upon the table to be passed about as opposed to just being ladled out from the pots in which it was cooked. These were indeed special meals.

At the meal, roast beef consumption was strictly regulated by fiat. Any complaints of unsatisfied hunger were referred to the potato and vegetable bowls for satisfaction. This by design left my mom with the raw materials she needed for a week's worth of future meals. Mom worked miracles with leftovers. I'm sure as she stared at that small brown nub of overdone beef, a single juice stained strand of butchers twine holding it upright, she fantasized about its future. What promise it held. Another sit down dinner perhaps, sandwiches to be packed off to school, roast beef hash, beef and barley soup, chipped beef on toast, deviled beef, beef ala king, oh, the possibilities were endless.

Alas, on this occasion, it was not to be. On the third trip back to the dining room while clearing off the table, my mother let out a blood curdling shriek. I thought a burglar must have broken into the house or a snake had gotten in again through the crawl space. My brother Brian and I rushed into the dining room to find my mother frozen in place, one hand clasped over her mouth, tears welling up in her eyes as she pointed at the platter on the table. It was gone. The lovely aroma still hung in the air but the leftover roast beef was gone. A small pool of juices and a short piece of soggy twine were all that remained. Before we could comprehend what had happened, my mother had weighed the evidence, formed several hypotheses and solved the mystery. Looking around the room she exclaimed, "Where is that damn dog?"

Me, on floor, Brian and Tipsy

Tipsy was the family dog, and dog food being expensive, I'm sure he was on a restricted diet like the rest of the Durst household. Although a very well behaved dog, apparently instinct got the better of him and he made a play for the beef. Even so, it was shocking to hear my mother curse, but especially at Tipsy. Truth be known, mom loved that dog and Tipsy was probably closer to mom than us kids. Like all kids who promise to feed and take care of a puppy if their parents will only let them have one, we quickly abandoned all care and feeding of Tipsy within three days of bringing him home. Mom took over, and Tipsy quickly became her dog. Mom loved that animal, but in just a moment, that dog was gonna get some tough love.

My mother went running outside looking for Tipsy. She spotted him in the corner of the backyard chewing on his purloined prize. As my mother approached, Tipsy looked up and actually started wagging his tail. Now I felt bad for my mom and the loss of her prized beef, but I felt worse for that dog. I don't believe mom had ever said a harsh word to that creature much less applied any corporal punishment to the animal. I don't think Tipsy had any idea what was heading his way. You see, us kids clearly knew what was happening when mom came at us in a sort of fast stumbling jog as she tried to close the distance between us and her as quickly as possible but also have one of her shoes removed by the time she got to us so she could more efficiently apply the lesson she wanted us to learn.

I can imagine Tipsy was thinking: "Oh here comes that nice lady that feeds me and boy this food she made for me here is the best ever. Oh look, she's taking off her shoe. She must want to play fetch, or maybe tug of war. I love that. Hey nice lady, do you want me to chase the slipper for you? Maybe we can play..., hey!, hey!, hey!, what the hell!, ow!, ow!, ow!, what are ya' doing?!!!"

Tipsy spent two weeks living outside. My mother, not to be deterred, picked up the chewed slimy piece of roast beef, tears streaming down her cheeks, and went inside and washed it off and we still ate it. I can remember taking those roast beef sandwiches to school, opening them up before I ate them and clearly seeing bite marks in the slices of beef. Some residual sand added a bit of crunch, but it was better than going hungry.

So with a constant hunger, lunch quickly became my favorite part of the school day. Besides getting a chance to eat, it was also a reprieve from the nuns as they went next door to the convent to have their lunches leaving us in the custody of Mr. And Mrs. Walters who ran the school cafeteria. The treat of treats was to be able to buy your lunch which happened only vary rarely for me. The Walters put out what looked like to me a wonderful smorgasbord of hamburgers, fries, fried chicken, mashed potatoes, salad, cakes, pies and drinks, all the food we never got to eat at home. Unfortunately, I never got to eat it at school either as all those items had a price tag attached. When I got money for lunch, I got thirty cents which got you a hamburger and a drink. fifty cents got you a burger, fries and a drink. If I had any fries with my burger they were nicked from a friend. And although I can clearly see to this day that chocolate cake wrapped in plastic, available at the very end of the cafeteria line, I'm afraid I am unable to describe here how it tasted.

Now that of course was a treat. Ninety nine percent of the time I was brown bagging it. I remember watching other kids unpacking their brown bags and I was amazed. Yes out came a sandwich usually, but like magicians reaching into top hats they would continue to pull out other items. Bags of chips and pretzels, cookies, snack cakes would appear as well as small tins of chocolate pudding and even napkins.

Inside my brown bag there contained one item and one item only, a ham sandwich. But calling it a ham sandwich might be a bit misleading. At the very least it was a generous description.

My mother used to buy quarter pounds of boiled ham at Val's market and make them slice it on the thinnest setting that the slicing machine offered. She wasn't satisfied until the butcher held up a slice and you could see through it. To make her "ham" sandwiches, my mother would take two slices of white Buttercrust bread, spread a thin veneer of Imperial margarine on both sides and then place one slice of ham on the bread ,trimming off any excess that hung over the sides and returning that to the package to be used again. The sandwich was then cut, wrapped in wax paper and put in the proverbial brown bag and sent with us to school. I think there were even some times when my mother was running so low on ham that she simply took the last slice and rubbed it on the bread to make the four sandwiches she needed for us kids. If my mother would have had to comply with today's food labeling laws, she would have had to label these things "Bread and Margarine sandwich with ham flavoring added, contains 2% or less of the following ingredients: ham"

But still lunch was my favorite period. We got away from the nuns and Colonel Good, and we did eat. We could socialize a while with our friends and could talk to each other without fear of reprisal.

The next best period was not a period at all but end of the day dismissal. At 2:45pm the big electric bell would ring in every building announcing the end of day. At 2:50pm the bell would ring again announcing that walkers could now leave. The 2:55 bell released the bikers and at 3pm those that were picked up by car could now head to the parking lot to find their parents.

Our gang were all either walkers or bikers. In the seven years of going to St. Cecelia's I cannot remember ever being dropped off or picked up at school by car, although I'm sure it must have happened. Even during a tropical storm, it was only rain and wind, so we were suited up in our yellow rain slickers and hats and sent on our way. The school was only about four miles away and it never dawned on us that we would need or want a ride.

The truth is that walking or riding our bikes to school gave us an enormous amount of freedom that we would never dream of giving up. Brian and I would cut across the YMCA field to meet up with Mike and Guy Keenan and then head toward St. Cecelia's often picking up Ron Grimes and Jeff Irwin as we passed their houses. We cut through back yards eating oranges, tangerines and kumquats along the way, and if we had a few coins in our pocket, we would stop by the Mister Donut before heading down to class.

On the way home, we cut across the Glen Oaks Golf Course located across the street from the school and between us and our home neighborhoods. The golf course was a blessing despite the fact that none of us played the game or knew the first thing about it. It did however offer one of the more efficient means of financing all of our childhood adventures.

Cutting lawns with Mr. Keenan's lawn mower and collecting soda bottles for the five cent deposit were certainly solid moneymakers, but they did require a considerable amount of time investment and, in truth, it was hard work. In the lawn cutting business, we were really being paid as common laborers and as such our income was largely limited by the amount of time we had to labor and the going rate of said labor. The bottle collecting was a sort of piece work, and if we collected more we got paid more, but it was a limited resource. It didn't take long for us to pick the immediate neighborhood clean of bottles. And although new commodity was added to the resource by careless soda consumers, we mined our neighborhood thoroughly. It was a diminishing resource coveted by all the kids and the law of diminishing returns quickly kicked in.

Guy Keenan suggested we begin engaging in true commerce. Somehow, Guy had discovered that during the game of golf, many golf balls were lost on the course. That of course was no interest to the rest of us until he also revealed that the golfers would pay good money to get those balls back. Even the pro shop at the golf course would buy used balls in bulk. We even had permission to swim the water hazards on the course and collect the lost balls. We now had demand and simply needed supply.

On the way home from school, we would work all the holes that ran alongside the streets we were traveling. We would collect a fair number of balls in the "roughs" and then search the edges of the water holes coming up with still more lost balls. On Saturdays we would "borrow" Frank Keenan's dive gear and use snorkel and mask to search the deeper parts of the water hazards. Business was good, but soon word got out to the other neighborhood boys. We had competition, and the law of diminishing returns kicked in again. Then, a stroke of pure genius.

One day while working the rough near a long par five, we were almost hit by several balls as they came flying in from downrange. Seeing no one close, we saw no reason not to grab the balls and throw them into our buckets. We then went hole to hole waiting for the balls to be hit to us, throwing them in our bucket and heading for another hole.

In all honesty we knew it was wrong and it caught up with us. It didn't take the pro shop or the patrons long to figure out that we were trying to sell them their own balls back the same day they lost them. We were forced to forfeit our inventories and were banned from the course.

Back at school, the weather was warming up, school was winding down and all of our thoughts were turning to summer vacation.

mmer vacations were anticipated with great enthusiasm

The Summer

We lived our summers in the two to three mile radius that was centered on our house, located at 1550 Lotus Path. The neighborhood consisted of a series of residential streets that ran off perpendicular from Lake Ave and all the streets terminated as cul de sacs as they met "The Creek" that ran alongside the back property line of the YMCA playing fields. There was Magnolia Ave., Lotus Path, Budleigh St. and Jeffords street going north to south. Hamrick Lumber Yard sat on Lake Ave. opposite Magnolia and at the end of Jeffords St. the creek partially dumped into a small body of water surrounded by woods. We dubbed this part of our domain "Finger Forest" for the three huge evergreen trees that dominated the west side of the pond. There was one huge tree bracketed by two smaller conifers that made the three look like they were expressing a common vulgar hand gesture.

A nursing home, whose parking lot bordered on the forest was to the west. The nursing home was actually one of the first ALFs (Assisted Living Facilities) that would soon become prolific across Florida as northern retirees would later flood the state earning it its nickname as "God's Waiting Room", long before the more conventional moniker of Sunshine State was adopted. We loved the ALF because it had an old fashioned ice cream parlor in it that we loved to visit, but our fondness for the place had nothing to do with the ice cream.

The ALF and the YMCA fronted Highland Ave. The Keenans lived on the opposite side of Highland and in the neighborhoods behind them you would find the homes of Jeff Irwin, Ron Grimes and other members of our gang. Beyond those neighborhoods was St. Cecelia's School.

This was our world, a world that could be traversed by foot in less than an hour, quicker on our bikes and more slowly, but much more stealthily by accessing the series of underground storm water pipes that crisscrossed our domain and of which the creek was really just an open section of that same system. We would occasionally venture further afield, taking our bikes to Clearwater Beach at least once a week to swim, fish and hang out with the hippies that lived underneath Pier 60.

Those trips to the beach were big events. We would strap our fishing poles upright onto the backs of our bikes looking as if we had huge whip antennas, and we filled our backpacks with fishing tackle, cast nets and every once in a while a few cans of beer if we were able to steal them from Mr. Keenan's cooler after he returned from a fishing trip out in the Gulf.

The fishing in and around Clearwater was amazing back then. I have heard tell that in the Fifties and Sixties that they would actually book fishing trips for the Yankees to come down and specifically fish the bridges. Our favorite spots were the old bridge from Clearwater Beach to Sand Key, gaining access by sneaking through the old Hilton hotel pretending to be guests to get to the beach behind. Even in the early Seventies, the fishing was incredible. Mackerel and even Kingfish ran heavily through that pass, and snook, redfish and trout could be caught at any time.

There were no seasons or limits back then, and if there had been, we would have ignored them. Behind the Gulfview Inn, a hotel that Mr. Keenan had built which we felt somehow gave us the right to use the property and the pool anytime we wanted, lay a canal that led to Clearwater Bay. At almost any time of the year, but especially during the spring, this canal would be loaded with mullet, so much so that the water appeared to be in a constant boil and was so clear you could see the fish several feet down. Here we would spend hours harvesting the vegetarian fish on bread balls (they will not hit a live bait) or snagging the fish by attaching huge treble hooks to our lines and jerking them through the water. Several fish houses on the beach would buy the mullet from us providing another financial resource for the group which was certainly more fun than cutting lawns.

But recreation and finance were not the only activities that the beach provided. There was a lot of education to be had, but it was certainly not from any teachers our parents or our more conventional instructors at St. Cecelia's would have approved.

Big Pier 60 stuck out from Clearwater Beach like a splintered concrete finger testing the waters of the Gulf of Mexico. It was touted as one of the big attractions in the area. Billboards and ads on the placemats of local restaurants encouraged tourists to "SEE BIG PIER 60!" and patronize the pier. Here a few dollars could buy you entrance, some bait and pole rental so you could squeeze in between dozens of other anglers, thankfully ignorant of the riches in the backwaters, and spend several hours of your vacation untangling your lines from the poles of other hapless Yankees visiting for the winter.

The real attraction was underneath the pier. In the early days , before the ordinance Nazis starting banning just about every activity on the beach accept breathing, (and now with global warming and CO2 emissions that's probably next), there were no laws against camping on the beach, sleeping on the beach, or for that matter, living on the beach. A group of hippies took up living under the pier and had quite a community going much to the chagrin of the more upstanding members of the community.

We thought the hippies were great. The span of the pier probably straddled as much land mass as it did water and underneath this pier the hippies built their homes. Sand walls were built to keep the cops from flashing their lights in at night and additional walls divided the living spaces of hippy couples. Despite stiff sea breezes, the smell of burnt rope hung omnipresent in the air, and although it would only be a few years hence that we would start burning a little rope of our own, at this point we were completely ignorant of its origin.

The hippy girls were our favorite. Up until very recently, we had no interest in girls whatsoever. I mean why? They didn't like to fight, they didn't like to build forts, and they thought it was "gross" if you didn't have a bath for a week. But slowly, questions were being circulated among the group of us boys about these strange creatures, who had always been all around us, but just now started occupying more and more of our thoughts.

These thoughts would pop into my head at the weirdest times. While fishing with Mike on a seawall, I would, just out of the blue, blurt out "I think Ann Walters smells good!" Mike would look at me like I had just thrown up on myself, take a few steps away from me, and quickly return to the fishing.

Roger Murphy brought up the question of what girls wear underneath their uniforms at school. I hadn't really thought about it much, but now that Roger had mentioned it, it was all I could think of. It soon became a topic of constant speculation as contraptions with straps begin to appear beneath our female classmates shirts. We soon found out that these were bras and speculation began about why those were now making an appearance.

One day, Roger Murphy brought in one of his older sister's bras to school and for twenty five cents, we got to touch it. We all went behind the cafeteria after lunch and Roger brought it out. He had it in a paper bag and when he reached in and pulled the contraption out, it seemed enormous.

How would one of these things ever fit on a girl? We paid our money and passed it around, and although the entire transaction was so innocent it could have been completed by mail, it did seem wrong and a little dirty. Of course being Catholic, we dutifully began feeling guilty immediately.

Charles Hall took it to another level. Charles showed up at school one day and had small mirrors glued to the top of his shoes. "What the hell are those for?" I asked. Charles replied, "Just watch and stand right next to me." Charles took me with him as he slowly walked up behind a group of girls on the playground. For some reason he was standing very, very close to them. I couldn't figure out what his game was. He gave me a wink and then started nodding down to his shoes. As I glanced at his shoes I could see that the mirror reflected up the girls skirt and you could see what was underneath.

My heart almost stopped as I realized what I was looking at and it scared me to death. I turned and ran and Charles ran after me. "Hey what's the matter? Didn't you see?" he asked excitedly. "Yea, yea, I saw", I said. "Isn't it great?" Charles continued, "I'm selling these things for 50 cents plus I've written down instructions on how to approach girls. You want one?" I declined. The bra was bad enough, but this was definitely wrong. My instincts were later born out when Sister

Regina Reilly noticed Charles suspiciously moving from one group of girls to another and figured it out. Charles was whisked off the playground by his ear, forced to write on the blackboard five hundred times "I will not look up girl's skirts", and required to go to confession every day for two weeks. He was also compelled to give up his customer list resulting in similar punishments for all his clients. Except for the depravity of it, it was kind of too bad because, judging by the number of kids attending detention and daily confession, Charles had been doing very well with his invention.

Now the girls at Pier 60 were in truth not girls at all but young women, and they were young women who liked to wear as little clothing as possible. It was impossible for a boy who was just beginning to enter puberty not to be attracted to the pier. We talked to the hippie boys, but were still just too terrified of the opposite sex to speak to the girls. We just ogled them instead, unable to form any coherent words when they were present.

Our hippy buddy Charley noticed this predicament and caught me ogling his girlfriend. "Hey, you like my old lady do ya'?" Charley asked with a smile. My eye shot away from her and straight back to Charley. I was terrified. Was he going to beat me up for looking at his girl? Maybe he would just kill me and bury me here beneath the pier never to be heard from again. "Hey it's okay little brother", he said. "She's a good looking chick isn't she? Do you have a chick of your own?"

I told Charley that no, I did not have a chick of my own and I'm not completely sure why, but I began to tell Charley about my recent infatuation with girls, how they had been occupying more and more of my thoughts and I simply did not know what to do about it.

"You got a chick you dig, man?" he asked. I hadn't really thought about girls in particular, that is in terms of a particular girl, but yea, if truth be told I did have one and her name was Anne Walters. I continued to bare my soul to my hippy friend telling him that I didn't know what to say to Ann and that every time I got near her I would get tongue tied and either nothing would come out or something so stupid that everyone within earshot would erupt in laughter.

Charley seemed to understand. "Hey Sandy, come on over here". Charley's old lady Sandy started heading for where we were sitting. She approached wearing Daisy Duke shorts long before Daisy hit the small screen and a bikini top that clearly answered the question of size inspired by Roger Murphy's sister's bra. "Kevin here doesn't know how to approach his girl. Tell him how we met baby." Sandy began talking about being at an outdoor concert, dancing with some friends, how Charley was with some friends, that they had met at a protest meeting a few months back, then they didn't see each other for a while and then…"no, no no, baby", Charley interjected, "tell him how we got *together*."

They both started smiling and then giggling and then they started kissing. Charley's hand found its way to that bikini top and then the other was heading for Daisy Dukes. I started getting uncomfortable and began to leave when they broke it off. "Oh no, no hang on. Sit down", Sandy said. "Let me tell you what happened. Charley was…well, baby, why don't you tell the story. You tell it better." Then Charley picked up the story. "Well hey man, it was no big deal. I just walked up to Sandy and grabbed her ass like this (he reached out and grabbed Sandy's ass) and said, hey man, I think you're far out. Those jeans look great on you, but they'd look better lying on my bedroom floor." They both started giggling again. Sandy said, "after that, I just knew he was the man for me, and we've been together ever since." Charley concluded, "So you see, just go up to your girl, grab her firmly by the ass and tell her how you feel." Sandy added, "It worked with me." And then she got up and went bouncing down the beach toward the volleyball nets.

This advice was a bit confusing. It didn't really seem right. It definitely conflicted with the advice about girls that Father Bueller had given me, but there were some things here to consider. Father Bueller's advice did seem to make sense, and it certainly wasn't as scary as this advice. However, Father Bueller did not have a girlfriend and Charley not only had a girlfriend, he had a very hot girlfriend. And not only that, but this hot girlfriend was telling me clearly that this was good advice and it worked on her. It was hard to tell which way to go.

I was suspended from school for a week. I had to write, "I will not grab the girls" one thousand times on the chalkboard and I had detention every day with Father Burkhoffer, a German priest who I'm sure had been a Nazi SS officer before taking his vows. I never spoke to Anne Walters again.

Although going to the beach and fishing occupied a fair portion of our time, during the summer our primary activities and the lion's share of our energies went into the Martial Arts. Now, it's not what you're probably thinking. We did not all take karate lessons together or all belong to the same dojo to learn Tae Kwan Do or even Ju Jitsu, not that those endeavors wouldn't have been a better use of our three month sabbatical from St. Cecelia's. No, what we did was go to war with the other kids in our neighborhood.

Forts, War and being Boys

In the two mile or so radius of our house there were probably three or four other groups of kids who hung out together like I hung out with my group. Well, it doesn't take long for five or six boys hanging out together to decide that they need something to hang out in, and so you start building forts. Now I don't know why they aren't "clubhouses", or "hangouts", but they're not. They're forts. The structures are designed for fighting, amongst ourselves and with other boys. ADD, ADHD, and all the other childhood anxiety disorders hadn't been invented yet. Neither had all the miracle cures for active children like Ritalin and the plethora of other psychotropic drugs been introduced to save America's children, so we just did what came naturally.

So believe it or not, groups of boys getting together making weapons and fighting amongst themselves, fighting with others, building forts to defend and attack, was actually considered normal, and if not encouraged, at least not discouraged as long as we heeded the age old motherly admonition not to "put somebody's eye out". I only remember one serious injury and as it turned out, Chuck was a pretty bright guy and he ended up going into law, which is certainly not a field that requires that you have ten fingers.

But in reality, we were simply products of our upbringing. Things considered too dangerous now were activities boys were expected to do. Even the toys we were given as kids were designed first and foremost for fun with safety as an afterthought if it was given any thought at all.

One of the first highly prized Christmas presents of  boyhood was to get a Gilbert Chemistry set. This was one of the ultimate "boy presents" ranking right up there with a Red Ryder BB gun with compass in the stock. I got my first one at age seven and was it ever a beauty. The set had test tubes, an alcohol fueled Bunsen burner and forty different bottles of chemicals including ammonium nitrate (this was the primary ingredient used to blow up the Murrah federal building in Oklahoma City), extremely flammable potassium permanganate, potassium chloride, sulfur and a couple dozen other chemicals designed for good clean fun. It even carried the Good Housekeeping Seal of Approval so you know it was a wholesome product. This kit today would immediately get you a spot on the Terrorist Watch List, but we were actually encouraged to spend hours mixing all this stuff together to see what happened.

"Mom were bored, there's nothing to do". We'd be told, "Get your chemistry set out and make something". Okay, well, that sounded like fun. "But Mom, I'm going to need a bottle of rubbing alcohol and some matches." My irritated mother would reply, "There's alcohol in the medicine cabinet and matches above the stove, now go to your room and get out of my hair".

Incredibly, one of the first experiments the manufacturers of this fine product encouraged you to do was: CHAPTER 1: EXPLOSIVES. Although I don't remember everything that was covered in that instruction manual, it wouldn't surprise me today if Chapter 10 was titled, FUN WITH METHAMPHETAMINES.

GILBERT CHEMISTRY   5

EXPERIMENT 1—How to make an explosive mixture

Mix thoroughly 1 measure of sulphur, 1 measure of powdered charcoal and 2 measures of potassium nitrate on glazed paper, but do not grind or rub the mixture. Then put the mixture on an old pan, and, standing off at a suitable distance, out of doors, being careful so as not to burn the hand or face, drop a lighted match on the mixture. Note the sudden flash and puff of smoke. Gunpowder is made from such a mixture, and is probably the longest known explosive. The potassium nitrate acts as an oxidizing agent, evolving oxygen on heating to burn the sulphur to sulphur dioxide and the powdered charcoal to carbon dioxide. *Do not attempt to perform this experiment with proportions of chemicals larger than those stated above.*

We made our first black powder gunpowder sitting at our desks with potassium nitrate, sulfur and charcoal and then placed a match to it to watch it burn up in a flash (as directed in the manual). I can't imagine how much of that stuff I inhaled and the only admonishment from my parents was to "Open up a window you're stinking up the house!" Incredibly, the manual warned that this experiment should only be done in small amounts as it was extremely dangerous if mixed in larger batches. Of course this only served to open up in our minds all the possibilities of what this substance in quantity could do. Thank God we never figured out what the ancient Chinese did and started compacting this powder into small tubes and then igniting it with a fuse. If we had, I would now be typing this memoir, not with a keyboard, but with voice recognition software.

Other great dangerous toys we had were a Thingmaker. This was a kit where you could make your own rubber toys by pouring molten rubber into die cast metal molds, allowing it to cool (that was a key part of the instructions, allowing it to cool), and then cracking the molds open to find the rubber worms, snakes bugs and other critters you had created. This was an activity considered safe for all ages. I can remember at six or seven using this kit with my four and five year old sisters. Here's how it worked.

Included in the kit was an open face electric hotplate, a utensil that looked like a soup ladle with a flat bottom, and a package of small rubber pellets in various colors. Children were instructed to plug in the hotplate until glowing red and place the ladle on the plate. Then simply add the pellets of the desired color to the ladle and wait until fully melted, about fifteen minutes or four hundred degrees Fahrenheit. Now in all fairness Mattel did recommend that asbestos safety gloves should be worn, but not included (item sold separately).

Once the molten rubber was ready, youngsters were then instructed to pour the molten rubber into small holes at the top of the metal molds, of course being careful not to spill any molten rubber outside of the molds.

Ask any parents about the ability of young children to pour milk from a pitcher into a glass, much less molten rubber from a flimsy ladle into small holes, and you'll know that the designers of this product never had kids. The rubber spilled onto our desks burning the Formica, spilled onto the hotplate itself causing, in essence, micro tire fires with black smoke billowing into the air causing us to choke on the fumes and our eyes to water. Of course we did this directly under our windows which made a curtain fire not just a possibility but a dead certainty.

At any one time, during the height of popularity of this product, about a quarter of my class would show up at school with bandaged hands or fingers. Amazingly my parents never blamed the toys. It was always our fault. Somehow I was responsible for my sister's burnt hands because a five year old didn't have the dexterity to work with molten rubber while manufacturing her own play toys.

And don't think the toymakers left the girls out of this fun. My sister had one of the first Easy Bake Ovens. This product first hit the market, ostensibly, to teach young American girls how to be future Suzy Homemakers by baking tiny cakes and cookies in a plastic box using a light bulb as a heat source. Although I understand that latter models of the oven used a common one hundred watt bulb as a heat source, the original oven used something like a ten thousand watt infrared heat lamp and would give you a nasty burn by just walking too close to it. Again, asbestos gloves were recommended.

But to be completely truthful, the toys of my childhood were really just sissified shadows of the truly great toys of my father and grandfathers childhood. My Thingmaker was, in essence, a watered down version of the original childhood toy known as The Gilbert Kaster Kit. In this little beauty, boys were encouraged to make their own toy soldiers. That sounds fine until you realize that to do this, boys were required to set up their own *lead smelting* operation in their bedrooms. Instead

of rubber, you melted down small ingots of lead and then poured *molten, freakin' lead* into the molds.

I just recently read that the EPA, much to the chagrin of the gun owning community, just shut down the last commercial lead smelting operation in the United States because of the toxicity of these operations. But in 1950's America, tens of thousands of kids all across the fruited plain, running their very own miniature, unregulated lead smelting operations, didn't even raise an eyebrow. Ahh, the good old days.

But the Best was the Gilbert Atomic Energy Lab. This was obviously introduced in the spirit of, "Whatever doesn't kill you makes you stronger", and by God we're going to make some strong boys.

This kit actually contained radioactive uranium, and radium (which is many times more radioactive than uranium) and the kit encouraged kids to conduct numerous nuclear experiments. The kit also included a working Geiger counter, I suppose so you could accurately measure the dose of radiation your child was receiving on a daily basis. The after school fun would have been endless.

"Johnny, shut down your atomic reaction and come to the table, dinner is ready. And make sure to put your plutonium in a safe place so the cat doesn't eat it." Dad would chime in "Listen to your mother Johnny. Put that plutonium where the cat can't get it. That damn animal is shedding hair all over the place."

Incredibly, if you misplaced your radioactive materials, or simply needed more for bigger better experiments, you could simply send in a coupon and the Gilbert Company would happily mail you more nuclear materials. (Just pay separate shipping and handling).

RADIOACTIVE SOURCE REPLACEMENT

The radioactive sources in your Gilbert Atomic Energy Lab will, in a period ranging from 1 to 50 years, deteriorate with time. Therefore, when replacement of your Alpha, Beta, Gamma or Cloud Chamber sources is required (see inside back cover of this manual) fill in the coupon below and send it to The A. C. Gilbert Company. You will be notified as to cost and mailing.

IMPORTANT!

NO REQUEST FOR RADIOACTIVE SOURCE RE-PLACEMENT CAN BE HONORED BY THE A. C. GILBERT COMPANY UNLESS IT IS ACCOMPANIED BY THE COUPON BELOW. KEEP THIS SHEET IN A SAFE PLACE, PREFERABLY WITH THE MANUAL OR WITH THE ATOMIC ENERGY LAB ITSELF.

So when we weren't combining incredibly dangerous chemicals together and lighting them on fire or playing with four hundred degree molten rubber lava, we were building forts.

The Fort

The final fort we ended up building eventually became a thirteen room three story structure with trap doors between the floors and tunnels underneath that ran into our yard and also under the YMCA fence and into the Y field. A series of spider holes dug into the creek bank served as a sort of picket line for any enemy forces that might be approaching. As the summer progressed, our group became the dominant force in the neighborhood. It wasn't due to our military prowess, although we did try to watch at least two to three reruns of Hogan's Heroes every week just to stay sharp. No, as in real life geo politics itself, it came down to one thing and one thing only: resources.

"The Fort" at the height of construction. One level is below ground with tunnels extending into our yard and YMCA Field opposite the fort.

Ron, Me and Guy working on the fort. You can just see my two sisters squeezing in the background.

Our first resource was the Hamrick Lumber Mill. In the early days of Clearwater, like many young towns, growth took precedence over zoning considerations and homes sprung up alongside commercial endeavors and vice versa. At the top of our street, surrounded by houses on all sides, was a lumber yard and truss building factory. Later in life as teenagers, this would provide us with convenient summertime and after school employment, but for now it provided us with the most valuable resource for fort construction, scrap wood.

Located just outside the yard office was a massive commercial dumpster where the scraps from the day's production were placed. Each day we found new treasures, and in the spirit of an old world chef who doesn't decide what to make for dinner until he sees what's fresh at the market, the design of our fort flowed from what was available at the yard. Somedays, it was hundreds of narrow strips of plywood too small for a contractor, but perfect in quantity to make a wall or a door for the fort. Other days it could be trimmings of 2x4s to make the perfect door frame or scrap pieces of siding leftover from a custom job.

Getting the wood from inside the bin down to the ground and loaded on to the carts was always a lot of work. Mike Keenan came up with an innovative solution. Instead of throwing each piece out separately, Mike found an old wide plank and leaned it against the side of the dumpster and slid the wood down in quantity, genius! This sped up wood collection considerably, but unfortunately it dawned on Mike that when he was finished sliding the wood down, he could then slide himself down the same plank.

Good thought, but perhaps not completely thought through. You see, that plank didn't exactly have a cabinet grade finish on it and as Mike slid down and picked up speed, a large sliver, more like a broom handle sized piece of that plank, came loose and went straight up his ass.

We all cringed in unison as we watched the impalement of our friend. But before we could get to him, he had jumped up, let out a blood curdling scream, and started a sort of fast waddle like run for home, running like he had, well, like he had a broom handle sized piece of wood shoved up his ass.

I suppose I should make a correction here. I guess we had two serious injuries during our fort building summers. But again, Mike ended up going into construction, a job where you certainly don't have to spend too much time sitting, so, there is that.

Kids heal quickly and Mike was soon back on the job with us, although he stayed on the outside of the scrap bin for the rest of his fort building days.

Of course wood was not the only resource we needed to build forts. You needed other things too, things people weren't throwing away like nails, shingles, screws, hinges, etc.. Our conventional approach to this problem was to earn some money to buy these items, something we were always encouraged to do. As I mentioned we would start out collecting pop bottles. Then like good entrepreneurs, we would take that capital and invest it. Seven pop bottles would get you enough to buy a gallon of gas. Then we would go get Mike's dad's lawn mower and that would be enough gas for five lawns at one dollar a lawn. We were rich! We thought we were clever parlaying a couple of pop bottles into five bucks. We soon found out that was nothing. We learned that there was a whole new world of finance out there just waiting to be discovered.

Before the Big Box stores, the only place to get what we needed was your local Ace Hardware store. There was one, I think the only one in town, and it was located just a block east of the school across from the Mister Donut where we would stop many mornings before class.

Often we would go to the store and just walk the aisles and look at all the cool stuff they had and dream of the things we could build with that gear. We would never have the money for that type of equipment. The few dollars we could scrap together was just enough for some nails, hinges and, on a good day, plastic sheathing.

One day Mike's dad Frank asked him to stop by after school and pick up a package for him at Ace. Frank was a local contractor who always had multiple projects going on around town and Mike and I usually rode our bikes home together after school, so I went with him. While we were at Ace, Mike and I pooled our meager resources and came up with $1.38 and decided to use that to buy some roofing nails to finish off the latest addition to the fort.

At the checkout line, Mike announced his name and asked for the package. When he saw the price written on the bag, it dawned on him that he certainly didn't have the money to pay for the goods. "I'm sorry ma'am," Mike said, "but my dad didn't give me any money to pay for this". The cashier looked at the bag and then said, "That's fine, you don't need money, we'll put it on your charge", she then pointed to our roofing nails and asked "do you want to put that on the charge too?" Mike and I looked at the nails, looked at the $1.38 in our hands and then both of us looked at the cashier and diffidently said "y-e-s???". The cashier grabbed the nails and put them in the bag and incredibly she asked "will there be anything else?" I looked at Mike, Mike looked at me, we both looked at the cashier and many years before Arnold Schwarzenegger made the line famous, we both said "We'll be back"

We rushed through the store grabbing nails, hinges, hammers, an electric drill and saw, all we could carry in one trip. Incredibly, I guess maybe because the charge account was under Kennan Construction, and we were buying construction stuff, the lady charged the whole lot and we walked out struggling to get all the stuff home. Deep down we knew something was not right, but how could you resist? Of course thirty days later we found out exactly how credit works and the concept of paying back over time. I still think I owe Mr. Keenan about fifteen more lawn cuts plus interest.

Of course resources alone are not enough. To defeat your enemy you had to have firepower superiority and that presented its own challenges. Like the ancients before us, you start with whatever you have at hand. First there was rocks, dirt clogs and sticks. These were okay at close range and the sticks were effective at hand to hand combat, especially when we began upgrading these weapons systems with sharpened points, and then

later, lashing on Mrs. Keenan's good steak knives
on the end forming spears. Unfortunately, these
weapon upgrades drew the attention of the
authorities and both Mrs. Keenan and my mother
intervened. Mrs. Keenan wanted her steak knives
back, but of more concern was the possibility of
having to deal with future puncture wounds in her
children.

My mother (not being an American and even to
her final days not having any appreciation at all of
the Second Amendment) called all the area
mothers together, from all the rival forts, for a
U.N. (United Neighborhood) Conference on
disarmament. The result was a draconian weapons
confiscation treaty agreed upon by all the mothers
denying all sides in the various and ongoing
conflicts access to sticks, spears, knifes and other
edged implements. Despite a universal outcry
among all the neighborhood factions, the jack
sandaled thugs carried out their tyrannical decree
searching bedrooms, forts, backpacks, and all
manner of places confiscating all objects that even
came close to falling within the description of the
contraband items to be seized. In their zeal to
trample the Second Amendment, the Fourth
Amendment was battered as no warrants were
issued naming the places to be searched and the
items to be seized. The Fifth Amendment took a
beating as boys were forced, under inhuman threat
of being denied their supper, to incriminate

themselves by admitting they had the contraband in question and where it could be found. And finally, worst of all, our basic First Amendment right to Free Speech and a Redress of Grievances was labeled "Backtalk" and "Lip" by these cruel draconian tyrants, and indeed we found out what countless populations throughout history had learned: when your right to bear arms is lost, all other rights will follow.

Paradoxically, the confiscation of these weapons actually lead to the proliferation of more weapons and a rapid acceleration in weapon design. As a matter of fact, something of an Arms Race broke out in the neighborhood with each fort trying to best the other until the contest reached a level of lethality where the Pinellas County Sherriff had to intervene to prevent a possible catastrophic event.

With the loss of the spears our group began to look at new, and hopefully more easily concealed weapons systems. We called our group P.O.M., Power of the Moon. Where did that name come from you ask? Were we particularly interested in astronomy and celestial bodies? Were we advocates of Wicca or New Age Druidism and believe that the moon has power over our lives and controls our destiny? Actually no. We found a flag laying in the creek that had a moon on it. None of the other groups had a flag. Flags were expensive. Flags were cool. So, we adopted the flag and in order for the whole thing to make sense, we needed a name that reflected the flag. Later we would find out that the more orthodox process of adopting a flag was to identify and name the group and then design a flag that represents that group. Live and learn.

Okay, so we had a flag. We had a Fort. We had an army of boys (six to ten we could field at any one time depending on key factors like, piano practice, chores or whether any particular part of your army was being grounded that week). Now we needed weapons. The race was on. Our first instinct was the weapon of giant slayers, the slingshot.

The first part was easy. There were many types of trees around the neighborhood and it didn't take long to find a branch with a good "Y" in it to cut down (with our pocketknife that we were allowed to carry in school, church, around town, wherever) and fashion a good slingshot frame. The next problem was the bands and the pouch.

My father was a big man. He was a big man at a time when the country wasn't yet eighty percent obese, so big was different. He had a hard time shopping at local department stores, and had to buy his clothes through a mail order company called Haband Clothiers. Now, I only mention this because Haband Clothiers was a critical supplier to the P.O.M weapons program.

Before the internet, mail order companies relied on sending out catalogs to potential consumers and oft times they would include samples. In the case of Haband, those would be fabric swatches of the various clothing items the company offered. One day in the mail arrived a large envelope from Haband announcing on the envelope that Haband was now carrying men's shoes and there were samples inside. Perfect. I opened the envelope and found small rectangular strips of brown, black and burgundy leather and descriptions of all the various footwear that could be had in the included sample styles. They made the perfect ammo pouch. I immediately sent the included Business Reply Envelope back to Haband telling them how happy I was that they carried shoes and planned to make a large order, could they send me samples of all their shoes. They did. Some heavy duty rubber bands acquired from Mom's office was the final piece (and yes, I did confess this to Father Bueller and I think the whole batch only cost me four Hail Mary's, two Our Fathers and a Glory be to God.) We now had all the components for new weapons systems.

As has happened countless times throughout history, the introduction of a revolutionary weapon, the crossbow, the musket, the machine gun, changes the course of history forever. So it was with our slingshots.

Their inaugural debut on the battle field was met with horror by the Ricky Buckner (I guess they couldn't find a flag to name themselves after) gang. What's the old adage? "Don't show up to a gunfight with a knife." Well Buckner and his minions shouldn't have showed up to a slingshot fight with rocks. We were waiting for them on the far side of the creek with superior position and superior firepower. We sat outside of their limited range and pelted them with impunity until they withdrew and we gave pursuit, raining rocks and stones on them until they retreated to the safety of their fort and locked the doors. We continued to barrage the fort with rocks and stones until we got bored and decided to retire. There wasn't any point in continuing. We had taken the field, humiliated the enemy, and forced them into retreat. Besides, Mom would have dinner ready in fifteen minutes and Hogan's Heroes came on at 6:30.

That's when the Arms Race began. Buckner and his gang showed up one day with store bought slingshots, devastating weapons called "wrist rockets" for the speed that they hurled a projectile. We responded with BB guns, they came back with pump pellet guns. We then responded with pyrotechnics, tying large numbers of "Black Cat" firecrackers together, forming a common fuse and then lighting them and shooting them with our slingshots at our opponents. Their response was bottle rockets to which we responded in kind sometimes having bottle rocket wars for hours with neither side hitting anything, but still great fun trying. Then finally we went too far.

The micro society that was our fort and gang wasn't totally martial in its makeup. Like all societies, there was also science and the arts. Our "arts" were generally limited to the graffiti we could get away with in and around town. That artistic side hit its zenith during a family vacation to New York City, culminating in our coup de gras of plastering the entire men's bathroom on the observation deck of the Empire State building with red and white "sunshine" stickers acquired from the bookstore of the college where my aunt was president.

In Science, we became quite advanced in rocketry. The Estes Corporation sold model rocket kits and supplies at the local Sears store in town. When we had a bit of extra money, we would buy one of the kits and several engines to go in them. The "engines" were cylindrical cardboard tubes packed with solid rocket fuel. The engines would fit into the bottom of the rockets and then you would insert a fuse into the nozzle, light it, and run like hell. The rocket was on a four foot guide rod and when the engine ignited, the rocket shot straight up

94

often over one thousand feet. It was recovered with a parachute. Always being scientific trailblazers, some of the rockets we bought had payload sections where you could put mice, lizards or other small creatures. (This was clearly pre PETA days). I can't clearly recall what scientific principle we were trying to prove by sending those poor creatures into the lower atmosphere, but it was always cool recovering the rocket to see if anything survived the flight.

Well, you probably know where this is going. Like the Chinese first, and then the Germans in World War II, it doesn't take young spirited boys long to figure out pretty quick that this could be a game changing weapon. Now I want to be clear, The Estes Corporation had no culpability in the events that were about to unfold. Even in an era well before people sued over spilled coffee, I can remember that on every rocket and every rocket engine it was printed: "Rockets Kill." "Never shoot a rocket at any person or object."

Two theories on warning labels and kids. It either keeps kids away from the activity in question (smart kids), or it gives eejits, (us), ideas. We decided to militarize our science project.

We set up a guide rod on the side of the fort and aimed it at the most likely route of approach for enemy forces. We stuffed the payload section full of Black Cat Firecrackers and ran a fuse down to the rocket engine. Our theory was that the rocket engine would ignite the fuse, and by the time the rocket got to its target, explode.

There was at this particular point in time a lull in military operations in the neighborhood. I'm not sure if it was the fatigue of war, or, like the old feudal kings who couldn't go to war during the harvest season because the peasants were out in the fields, it was because Little League Baseball had begun and kids were playing ball instead of fighting. Like a shiny new toy, we had to play with our new weapon so we decided a "test fire" was in order.

We mounted the guide rod on the back of the fort and decided we would shoot the rocket over past the YMCA Field and into a large tree in the Community Hospital Field. What could possibly go wrong?

Brian lit the fuse and ran for cover. We all watched from well behind the fort to see what would happen. The rocket took off, and with a high speed hiss, headed straight for the tree. The rocket hit the tree dead center with the engine still firing, then fell to the ground and sort of spun around and flopped about beneath the tree until the engine was spent. Disappointingly, the firecrackers never went off. This was a design problem we would have to address, but the rocket was cool and did exactly what we thought it would do.

As I mentioned, even though the show was in reruns when the gang and I first saw it, we were huge Hogan's Heroes fans. We loved the character of Colonel Hogan directing a band of witty, smart allied soldiers in covert missions against the hapless Germans. Dressed all in black with charcoaled faces, Hogan, Newkirk, Lebeau and the gang would go out and blow up bridges, derail trains and save French Underground Agents from the dreaded Gestapo. We loved it, and modeled many of our Fort exploits after Hogan's adventures.

So much so that every boy in our Fort was required to have a special set of clothing for performing "Missions". That outfit included a black stocking cap, black sweatshirt and black pants. In our black outfits, we would wander the neighborhood playing ding dong ditch it, stealing oranges from trees, putting firecrackers in mailboxes or whatever else we could define as being a "Mission". Today we probably wouldn't get fifty yards before being shot as Al Qaeda Terrorists.

Since it was getting dark, we decided to make the recovery of the rocket a "Mission". Brian, myself, Guy and Mike Keenan and Ron Grimes all donned our black gear, rubbed charcoal on our faces, and headed out toward the hospital. It never dawned on us that we might look just slightly suspicious, five guys dressed all in black, climbing over fences and trespassing on a medical facility.

It was like walking through ink on the way to the hospital, but there appeared to be a growing glowing in the distance. As we got closer to the tree, we realized that the rocket had started a fire in the field and it was spreading rapidly. We closed the distance quickly and gathered up handfuls of sand throwing it on the growing fire. Guy ran back to the house to get some buckets to draw water from the creek.

Just when we about had the fire under control, I looked up and realized we had an audience. In the parking lot there were four men and at least one of them was in uniform. They seemed to be pointing directly at us and the uniformed fellow was talking into a radio. Suddenly, all hell broke loose. The firecrackers that were in the rocket had finally been exposed to flame and they started popping off in rapid succession. It scared the hell out of us, but the guys in the parking lot, who had been watching five guys in black Ninja outfits putting out a fire, started diving for cover. I think they thought they were being fired upon. It was definitely time to go.

We squashed the last flame, left the rocket and headed back to the creek and the safety of the fort. Just a hundred yards or so into our retreat, the whole area lit up as if it was day, and the whoop, whoop, whoop of a helicopter could be heard overhead. We could hear sirens and see police lights in the distance. Brian yelled "They called the cops. Let's go!"

Now I can't understand why they had to involve the law. I mean it was only five guys dressed in black, trespassing on a medical facility loaded with drugs, starting a fire and then, as far as they knew, opening fire on the security guards. I mean really, was it necessary to bring in law enforcement?

As an interesting quirk, one of our neighbors was Gerry Coleman who just happened to be Sherriff of Pinellas County. He was immediately on the scene as he had a mild curiosity as to why his newest law enforcement asset, a helicopter with night vision and searchlights, was buzzing over his house and lighting up the neighborhood. We were in trouble. In the end though, it was actually Hogan's Heroes that saved us.

As we made our way back to the fort via the creek, I got caught in the spotlight several times and I could see police officers on the ground with flashlights nearby. Mike also got caught in the spotlight several times so the guys in the chopper knew they were chasing something. As we got near the fort I remembered the tunnels we had dug into the bank of the creek. So did Mike and Brian. We went underground and spent the next several hours listening as police combed all around. I even heard Gerry talking with my Mom who also had no idea what was going on and since it wasn't that late, she just assumed we were over at the Keenans.

After some time, the search wound down. The helicopter was recalled, the police cars receded and Gerry went back to the house. We apparently got away clean, almost. In the end, Gerry went over and investigated the fire, saw the rocket, knew about our Missions and put two and two together. He had a little chat with us and made a deal. He wouldn't tell our parents and we would swear off rockets as future offensive weapons. Sounded like a good deal to us. No harm no foul.

All War and no Play Makes Johnny a Dull Boy

In between our offensive operations is when we attended to our other activities such as biking down to the beach, camping on the islands and visiting our hippy friends on Pier 60. One of our favorite activities was all going to the Old Fashioned Ice Cream Parlor that was part of the ALF near Finger Forest.

There were two main places to get ice cream that fell within our world. The place we actually went to much more often and had a much better deal on ice cream was the Dairy Kurl on Gulf to Bay Blvd across from Crest Lake Park. This was a tiny ice cream shop with only outdoor seating, but small cones were only nine cents and large with a chocolate dip were twenty four cents. This was by far the best deal in town and much cheaper than the Old Fashioned Ice Cream Parlor, which was also only open sporadically a couple of days a week.

However, if word got out in the neighborhood that the Old Fashioned Ice Cream Parlor was open that day, we pulled out all the stops to make the trip, and word spread like wildfire among the neighborhood boys that the shop was open. If no money was in the coffers, we immediately went into bottle collecting mode, scouring the streets and trash cans of the neighborhood for soda bottles with a deposit on them to return for the five cent bounty they held. The ice cream was expensive. A cone was fifty cents and was actually smaller than the nine cent cone at Dairy Kurl. It wasn't particularly that good. For the cost of a cone here, we could get a quart of ice cream at the Farm Store that was much better. The other items, sodas, malts, shakes and sundaes were well outside of our financial reach. So why did we go to The Old Fashioned Ice Cream Parlor? Her name was Claudia.

Claudia was a nurse at the Assisted Living Facility that the ice cream parlor was a part of, and I suppose a couple of days a week she got Ice Cream duty. We were all in love with Claudia. She was, I would guess, in her late twenties, with an hourglass figure that was clearly revealed by the skin tight white nursing uniform that she wore. The uniform had a plunging neckline, enhanced by Claudia's God Given talents, stockings and a hemline that was clearly the high water mark for decency in the early Seventies. The uniform would later be made famous in such adult films as "Naughty Night Nurses", and "Revenge of the Naughty Night Nurses, (or so I have been told by others…ughum).

The best thing was that the Old Fashioned Ice Cream Parlor sold samples. For ten cents you could have a mini scoop in a small paper cup with a flat wooden mini- spoon. The Ice Cream Parlor was a sort of No Man's Land of the neighborhood, a place where an unspoken truce was always in effect and members of all the forts could come and go freely. I don't remember any of the boys in the neighborhood ever buying a whole cone. We always bought samples. And it wasn't a financial issue.

You see, at the shop, the barrels of ice cream were held in a low coffin style freezer where Claudia would have to steeply bend over and scoop the ice cream out, especially if that particular barrel was low. In the process a young boy's fantasies came true and we watched with laser like focus as the ice cream was scooped out, hoping that maybe she would drop it and have to start the whole process over again.

As we all sat there one day ordering sample after sample, I found myself drifting off into some sort of impossible fantasy. I awoke when I heard Claudia saying "We're out of chocolate chip. Kevin, we're out of chocolate chip." I snapped out of my mammary induced trance and just blurted out "CHOCOLATE TITS!" There was dead silence in the parlor. I looked at Mike and Guy who stood there with their mouths open. Did I really say that aloud? I turned to look at Brian who was standing there with a shocked look on his face. I had said it aloud. Oh my God! I'm finished. Claudia will tell my Mom and I'll never be allowed back again. She tell everyone, my teachers, the priests, I'll be banished for life. Claudia looked at me her eyes narrowing from disbelief into anger. Just then Brian, always quick on his feet, jumped in to save me. "Chocolate bits, he said chocolate bits, do you have anything with chocolate bits?" Claudia slowly closed the top to the ice cream freezer and handed me what was in the cup. "Okay boys, the show is over for today. I'm closing up early so I'll see you later." She directed us toward the door. As we left though, Claudia looked at me and I saw a slight grin creep across her face as she turned away. I realized there for the first time that maybe these things called girls weren't totally the alien creatures that I had feared they may be.

Well we were only a few weeks into this summer when our resources and weaponry gave us a sort of hegemony over the neighborhood and most of the serious challengers faded away. The summer started to drag on a bit, but then we overheard Father Bueller talking about going to Ireland. Brian and I began to start talking, fantasizing really, about how we could possibly go with him. Mom certainly didn't have the money and it seemed doubtful that we would be able to collect enough pop bottles, cut enough lawns or steal enough golf balls to bankroll two transatlantic voyages. Just as it seemed that all hope was lost, deliverance arrived driving a sky blue 1970 Chevy Nova.

The Deal

Although Father Bueller had his character flaws, he also had admirable character traits. He was certainly a man of integrity and particularly a man of his word. As a result, my brother Brian and I got a free trip to Ireland for the summer, I smuggled my first contraband across international borders, and the two of us very nearly spent the sixth and seventh grade respectively in a Jesuit school outside of Dublin. But I'm getting ahead of myself.

It goes back to the Quaaludes, or Soapers, I mentioned earlier. Father Bueller not only invented Doctor Shopping, he got very good at it. As it turned out, at any one time, FB could have six to eight active prescriptions going and he was not a man who could pace himself. Father Bueller had something of a problem with "luding out". This was a phenomenon where the Quaalude consumer would completely black out the next day and have absolutely no recollection of the events of the preceding twenty four hours. This may have explained FB's problem making it to weddings, but it was causing all sorts of other difficulties as well.

My mother decided that an intervention was necessary, and she was able to get the good father to turn over all his pills and the prescriptions. She would then disperse on an "as needed" basis.

The intervention was successful for about two days after which Father Bueller showed up at our house looking for the drugs. He made sure to come by between three and five pm, after we had gotten home from school, but before my mom got back from work.

I remember how Father Bueller would arrive at the house. You could clearly hear him approach in his sky blue 1970 Chevy Nova because Bueller only knew two speeds, stop and full. As I mentioned, we lived on Lotus Path, the last house on the right of a dead end street. The Clearwater YMCA backed up to our property, and the driveway to the house was perched at an almost forty five degree angle to the road on a hill where the house sat. The squeal of the brakes, followed by the scraping of metal as the Chevy bottomed out on the drive, announced his arrival.

Now it was not unusual for Father Bueller to stop by the house just about any time. Once he navigated the driveway and was able to throw the car into park, the vehicle would sit and diesel for upwards of three to five minutes as the incredibly abused engine tried to shut itself down. FB would be on the porch and headed through the door while the car still bucked, sputtered and cried in the drive. I don't ever remember the man knocking. He would simply throw the door open, head right for the stove, put on the kettle for tea and sit down at the flimsy folding apparatus that served as our kitchen table. He would then start chain smoking filterless Pall Mall cigarettes with a deliberateness that made you wonder if there was some sort of unspoken contest as to how quickly one could fill up an ash tray.

On this particular occasion, Brian and I returned from school to already find Bueller in the kitchen with an ashtray about quarter full indicating he had probably been there no more than twenty minutes. There was no greeting, no salutation, no inquiry as to our well-being, simply, "Lads, do you know where your Mum keeps the Soapers?"

Now of course we knew where Mom had them hiding. We also knew that giving them to Father Bueller was not a good idea.

You see, we had witnessed FB on a good old Soapers tear and it was not something either my brother or I wanted to see repeated. On one occasion, prior to my mother's intervention, the good Father stopped by our house after what by this time had become one of his fairly well known Soapers/Budweiser/Jameson goodwill tours of the parish.

Periodically Bueller would pop a couple of Soapers, wash them down with a few Buds, hop in the old blue Chevy and make the rounds of well-known St. Cecilia parishioners, usually the Irish crowd, the O' Conner's, Fitzgerald's, Spellisy's and others. Now I don't want you to think that Father Bueller was ethnocentric or discriminatory. It's just that he knew that at these addresses he would be offered a healthy portion of the third leg of his Soapers/Budweiser/Jameson trifecta and wouldn't have to resort to his own supplies. Later, when a healthy population of Greeks moved down from Tarpon Springs and joined the parish, Father Bueller discovered Ouzo. The Cubans from Miami introduced dark rum and a group of Polish parishioners from Chicago brought Vodka. Bueller quickly earned a reputation in the community as being something of an internationalist.

The last stop of the tour was almost always our house. On this particular occasion Bueller flew through the door late one afternoon to announce that he had arrived to do some work on the house.

Our house on Lotus Path was of a very peculiar design. After buying the house, we found out from the neighbors that it was actually built by the fellow we bought it from, a fact the seller did not disclose to my parents. The universal opinion of the neighbors was that the man had no idea what he was doing, an opinion that gained more and more credibility the longer we lived at that address. One of my mother's chief complaints, heard almost every day it rained, was that although the house had an attached garage, there was no door from the garage into the house. This day, Bueller arrived to correct this flaw.

Bueller burst through the front door to announce, "Lads, I'm here to put a door in for your mother", he proclaimed. "It's criminal that poor woman has to get soaked to the bone every time it rains, now we want to get this done before your mum gets home, so we have to get straight to the matter....But first, let's have a beer!"

Bueller stood there in the kitchen with two six packs of Budweiser tall boy cans hanging from each hand. A can missing from each pack allowed him to hold the five packs aloft in front of him like one would show off two lovely stringers of fresh caught fish. A mischievous grin crept across his face.   I honestly believe, in a case we would passionately make to our mother later that evening, that a fourteen and fifteen year old boy really had no power to intervene in the course of events that was soon to transpire.   FB was a priest, an authority figure we did not question, and we *assumed* he had discussed this construction project with my mother prior to arriving on site. And after all, it was a hot summer day and a couple of cold beers sounded pretty good.

With our thirst quenched, FB produced an 8 pound sledge hammer for himself and a couple of smaller framing hammers for us. With no regard for locating the electrical, plumbing, the underlying studs or even roughly marking the area to be demolished, Bueller gave the command to break through the wall.

 Brian and I now had two tall boy Buds in us as we attacked the plasterboard with relish. Bueller joined in, 8 pounder in one hand, Tall Boy Bud in the other. As he smashed out the wall area closest to the ceiling, my brother and I took out the lower parts. An encounter with an electrical wire was met with the command, "Rip it out lads, we'll put a new one in later." I cannot remember anyone ever turning off the electric service, but surely no one would have been that irresponsible.

After about an hour of this, and the consumption of the balance of the Budweiser, we had successfully smashed through the kitchen wall and could see through into the garage. Bueller was a little unsteady at this stage, so Brian crawled through to the other side to rip out the drywall in the garage

. As quickly as he began the project, Bueller called for a work stoppage. With a quick glance at his watch he said, "All right lads, that's good for today. I've a Novena to say, so I'm off." With that he was gone. Brian and I stood there amongst the wreckage a little confused, but also enjoying a pretty good Budweiser buzz. We were covered in drywall, plaster and dust as was the kitchen and garage. Just moments later, my mother arrived home from work.

I'll skip the details of what transpired after my mother's arrival home, suffice to say that she was completely unaware of the construction project we had been recruited for and in no way did she issue a Notice to Commence. Other than the application of some plastic sheathing, the project was put on indefinite hold. So were all our activities other than school and household chores for a month.

The second Bueller/Soaper incident really drove home the reality to me that it was probably a bad idea for FB to have too liberal an access to strong narcotics, not to mention strong drink.

As I mentioned earlier, we lived on a dead end street, the last house on the right. A creek, an open storm sewer really, that during heavy Florida rains turned into quite a torrent, ran along the side of our house between the end of the road and the back playing fields of the Clearwater YMCA. To get to the Y, we would cross the creek, climb the fence and go in through the back door. The front of the YMCA building faced Highland Ave.

At the end of our street, before coming to the creek, was a large storm sewer opening. During heavy rains, the water would rush down the street, sometimes backing up and collecting in knee, or even thigh deep, water after overwhelming the sewer grate. It didn't take long for a large amount of sediment to build up at the bottom of the cul-de-sac forming quite a sand berm.

We often joined other kids in the neighborhood and used the sand berm as a ramp to see if we could jump the creek on our bikes Evil Knievel style. Although we often had success clearing the creek when it was at normal levels, we could never get to the YMCA field as that side of the creek bank was a good ten feet higher than our street side. We never failed to keep trying though.

 Soccer was really the first "major" sport to come to Tampa. We were all Tampa Bay Rowdies fans and Rodney Marsh was our hero. It was with my mother, brother and two sisters returning from an evening Rowdies game that we saw an unusual incident at the bottom of our street. The road being a cul-de-sac, and us living at the end, the only people or cars you normally saw either belonged to us or our opposite neighbors.

 That evening, as we turned down Lotus Path, there were lights flashing, neighbors gathered and a beehive of activity happening right in front of our house. As we crept closer, there was clearly a police car, a fire truck and an ambulance, but no other vehicle. There were neighbors, some in bed clothes, gathered on our lawn as well as the lawn of our neighbor across the road. I even saw Mr. and Mrs. Voiland standing on the neighbor's lawn which was unusual as they lived a full block over. A hundred yards or so from our driveway, you could begin to make out a figure that was standing in front of the police car. He was difficult to discern at first as he was dressed all in black, but when he turned to face our oncoming car, the collar betrayed him and my mother gasped, "Good Lord it's Bueller"

Now my mother knew that the chances were pretty good that Father Bueller had been stopping by our house, as was his custom, at the end of one of his goodwill tours and he was probably fairly well nourished either by his own hand or was over served at one of his stops. Either way, the fact that he was standing in front of a police cruiser, and having some sort of interaction with law enforcement, was not a good thing. I think pure instinct kicked in and my mother went into denial mode. "Okay, when we pull into the driveway, everyone get out and go right into the house. Don't look at anyone; don't say anything, go inside and go straight to your rooms." Mom said it in her "Don't even think about questioning me on this" voice.

Well, I tried to obey my mother, but I just couldn't resist. I mean, it's a train wreck, right? You have to look. It's basic human instinct. Before my mother could shoo me inside and give me "the eye", I surveyed the scene. I took it in quickly, but every detail burned into my mind, the neighbors, the cops, fire, ambulance, Bueller. But something was missing. Where was his car?

Despite my mother's instructions, I happened to catch Father Bueller's eye before turning away from the scene and heading for the front door of our house. It hurt to turn away. After all he was a family friend, someone I was around all the time. I do have to admit I felt a little like Peter denying Christ when I broke eye contact and walked toward the door. But at the moment, Mom was Pontius Pilate, and she looked like she was more than willing to hand out thirty lashes to anyone who defied her now.

A few short steps from the house a horrendous crack broke through the subdued din of the neighbors gossiping and the officials officiating. The sound was that of sharp thunder, but the skies had been clear all night. The noise redirected my eyes. I had found the car.

The crack was the rather stout limb of a great granddaddy oak that, despite its considerable strength, could no longer bear the weight of a sky blue 1970 Chevy Nova. It appeared as though Bueller had easily accomplished what none of us neighborhood kids were able to do. He had easily cleared the creek, the extra ten foot on the opposite embankment, and what at a casual glance I estimated to be an additional fifteen feet. It appeared, except for the unfortunate location of that great Oak, he would have landed in the YMCA field and could have simply driven across the soccer pitch and turned on to Highland Ave. avoiding the entire messy business now unfolding at the bottom of my street altogether. Just bad luck really.

Incredibly, there were no arrests. No charges were filed and the Y really didn't make any scene at all about their oak tree. Of course those were different times.

In the early Seventies MADD didn't exist. Drunk driving was considered more of a roguish act than a crime and if a tree died you cut it up for firewood and people were happy for the fuel. Today, Bueller would have gotten a year in jail for drunk driving, the car would have been searched resulting in multiple felony charges for possession of multiple controlled substances, doctor shopping, and open container. Charges would have been filed for destruction of city property, county property and destruction of a protected species. The YMCA would have sued the church, city and county. Friends of the Earth would have extorted the diocese for tens of thousands, and several of the onlookers would have suffered trauma resulting in the manifestation of repressed memories of sexual abuse by a priest and would have filed multiple multi-million dollar lawsuits against the Church.

But as I said, it was a different time. The next day a wrecker came out and it was decided that it would actually be easier, and cause less damage to the vehicle, to pull the car back across the creek to our side. The wrecker did just that and other than some scratches, broken headlight, and a couple of dents I couldn't swear weren't there before, the old Nova wasn't in too bad a shape. It did have a flat rear tire that my brother offered to change.

Apparently, Bueller's explanation of the incident at the scene satisfied everyone involved. His story, and he stuck with it, was that he saw a light at the back of the YMCA and he thought it was a street lamp and that the road went all the way through.

Now of course Father Bueller had been down our road only ten thousand times over the last several years and I'm surprised that his car didn't automatically turn into our driveway. Of course the police didn't know that. Despite that, even when talking to us, he was defiant that he had done nothing wrong. Who knows what really happened, but judging by the trajectory to the tree and the angle of the sand berm at the bottom of the street, he must have been doing sixty when he hit the ramp. God does protect fools and small children.

As I said, defiant to the end, when my brother replaced the flat tire for Bueller, he insisted that the wheel was on backwards and Brian didn't know what he was doing. It wasn't. Bueller took the wheel off, put it on backwards, kind of tightened the lug nuts and drove off. The wheel fell off about hundred yards up the road. We all hurried inside the house and locked the doors.

So that was our history with Father Bueller and Soapers when he showed up looking for the stash that mom had hid.

But even that being said, my brother recognized an opportunity when he saw it. Father Bueller was leaving for Ireland in a week's time and would be returning the first week of August, which coincided perfectly with the remainder of our summer vacation. To add fuel to the fire, he had been teasing us mercilessly about taking us with him and we had been begging him to do so. We tried to convince him that we'd be no trouble and all he'd have to do was drop us off at our Aunt's in Dublin and pick us up at the end of the summer. We'd be no bother at all.

We had overheard our Mother talking to a friend of hers about Bueller's trip. Apparently, two wealthy parishioners, spinsters actually, were bankrolling this trip back to the old sod and Bueller was getting an all-expense paid trip back home if he agreed to play tour guide to these two old darlings. Bueller also knew an opportunity when he saw it, and managed to parlay the offer into First Class tickets on the new 747 to Europe, Five Star accommodations for the summer and a rental car for three months.

His joke to us was that he would take along my brother and me as his assistants, protégés, good altar boys that were considering a life in the priesthood and needed a summer internship in Ireland so they may be more receptive to the calling. When Bueller wanted to, he could really lay it on thick.

Well, I guess that's where any real deal starts. We had something Bueller wanted and he had something we wanted. Brian started the negotiations employing a minimalist strategy. He offered the bare minimum, knowing he would negotiate up, but hopefully not as far up as his adversary wanted. Brian opened with "I'll give you three Soapers now, two next week and the rest of the bottle when we get to Ireland." Bueller countered with an "ask for the world and settle for a continent" strategy. "I want all six bottles, and all the refill prescriptions" Brian countered with "half a bottle now, half a bottle next week, and a refill before we leave".

The offer/counteroffer now flew fast and furious. In the end, Bueller got the bulk of the pills, we got to fly business class to Ireland and so began a Summer my relatives in Ireland still talk about, my mother won't discuss and that we very nearly missed out on completely except for one critical detail that my brother managed to remember.

You see, like the hero in a classic Greek tragedy whose character flaw ultimately destroys him, the very goods comprising this transaction held the potential for its undoing. Now I want to be clear. It's not that we didn't trust Father Bueller or doubted his integrity.   We had an enormous amount of respect for him and he was universally considered a man of his word. But to keep his word, he had to actually remember that he gave it. We quickly realized that if we handed over this quantity of narcotics to FB, it would almost ensure that he would "lude out" and not remember a thing in the morning, or the morning after that depending on how carried away he got. This is where I saw my first exercise in contract law and its importance in commercial transactions.

Before Brian would hand over the pills, he took a sheet of loose leaf paper from his school notebook and scribbled out a quick "drugs for travel agreement" spelling out the goods to be delivered to FB and the services to be granted to "the lads" in return. Bueller quickly signed it. Brian signed on behalf of the both of us (I was a minor after all. And, yes, I know what you're thinking, and you're right. Brian was a minor too. The transaction involved a federally controlled substance that didn't belong to us, taken without consent from my mother, who was in possession of the pills illegally, to be given back to one party of this contract who originally came into possession of the narcotics by fraudulent means. How could one more illegality possibly matter?)

Well, as we predicted, our impromptu contract became indispensable in securing the deal.

When we finally saw the good Father several days later, we excitedly inquired about the details of the trip, when we'd be leaving, who was going, what we should pack, etc. He thought we were kidding and started joking back with us about how nice it was going to be in Ireland and how it was too bad we couldn't make it, love to have you along, we're going to have a great time, etc., etc., etc..

 When his teasing finally started to run out steam, Brian produced the contract. Bueller's smiling face slowly melted blank, then to consternation and then he just looked plain sick. Confusion hijacked his face. He clearly didn't remember. However, there were some facts here, and facts are stubborn things. The signature on the paper was his. He *had* come into possession of a large number of Quaaludes, and the date on the piece of paper fairly closely coincided with the last date he could remember.

Despite the gross illegality of the entire transaction, Bueller honored the agreement. He announced to my mother that after much soul searching, he decided that he had an obligation to take the lads to Ireland, so they could see their family, learn their heritage, get some European culture, etc, etc, etc. Mom bought it. It wasn't a hard sell. After all she got rid of us for an entire summer and it wasn't going to cost her a thing. Little did she know, nor did we, that getting there would be the simple part. Getting home would ultimately involve the diplomatic efforts of two countries, the Irish national police force, the Vatican, and the Irish council of Bishops.

Dublin

My mother was born and raised in a small village just south of the Irish capitol of Dublin. Dundrum at that time was a distinct small village well removed from the hustle and bustle of the largest city in the new republic. It has since become really just an extension of the city, but much of its charm lives on. My mother's ancestral home survives today, situated on the Main St., but now serving as an apothecary (drug store) and hardware shop.

My mother's sister, and my Aunt Rita, along with cousins Jim, John and Paula still lives just up the main road in an old stone house with a shale roof cozily ensconced on a small parcel of land behind Uncle Tom's Cabin, a favorite local pub.

Aunt Rita would have been a casting director's dream if called upon to produce a sweet elderly grandmother. Stout of frame and white of hair, with piercing blue eyes, you knew she was the sweetest of souls before she ever spoke a word. She was almost always attired in a simple flowered housecoat or if going out, unassuming but elegant wool skirt, a white blouse and tweed jacket. I'm sure the woman never wore a pair of pants in her life.

If any criticism could be leveled at her it was perhaps her proclivity to collect things. I would later realize that she was the first real hoarder I had ever met. She kept used tea bags to "moisten the garden" in a country where it rained two hundred and seventy five days a year. She kept all the newspapers she ever bought to light the fire. Fair enough, but in 1993, in a barn behind the house, I pulled a newspaper out of the *front* of an Everest like pile with the headline "Nixon Resigns".

Navigating her house was something of a challenge and actually as kids we found it fun as it was something of an obstacle course to get from the front door to the kitchen. That is, if you knew where the kitchen was. My aunt not only was a "collector", she also had a proclivity for rearranging things. I'm not talking about furniture here. She would rearrange entire rooms for apparently little or no reason, or at least none that the rest of the family could figure out. I remember the kitchen being in at least three different locations and in one case her kitchen changed locations, plumbing and all, in the course of three days.

Now, on that occasion, her son, and my cousin, Jim had just returned from a day in Dublin. On the way home, we stopped in Uncle Tom's cabin for a quick pint but in all honesty we ended up being criminally over served.

Fortunately it was only a short stumble from the pub to the house. We went through the front door and headed for the last known location of the bedroom that Jim and I were sharing. In our bedroom we found a sink, a large table and a gas stove. We actually ended up walking out of the house and back in twice, convinced we had taken a wrong turn despite the fact that Jim had spent his entire life in that house.

Jim's sister Paula woke us up in the morning with a disgusted look saying she would have breakfast in town and that we better get up quick before Aunt Rita woke and found us asleep on her mother's antique kitchen table.

The house has no address. More appropriately, it has a name, Mossvale Argnagle. A letter from anywhere in the world will arrive there with that simple notation. The river Dodder runs along the front side of the property requiring that visitors carefully navigate a narrow stone bridge to get to the house. At almost any time of the year in this cold, damp country, a steady stream of smoke can be seen coming out of the multiple chimney pots atop the stone chimney, the number of pots advertising to anyone who cares to count, the number of fireplaces in the home below.

The fuel for that fire was almost always peat. Peat is a geological precursor to coal, dug out of huge bogs throughout the country, stacked pallet like to dry and burned in almost every home on that windswept island.

Many years after this boyhood adventure in Ireland, I would return to live in my ancestral homeland, and for the first few months I lived with my Aunt Rita. Walking home on a cold, wet Irish evening, the aroma of the burning peat would welcome you back, invading your nostrils with its earthy, familiar smell well before you could see its source. More often than not, that smell would mix with the four or five pints of Guinness just consumed at Uncle Tom's. The two together would conspire to tease your appetite, antagonize your hunger and conjure up wonderful images of arriving home to find Aunt Rita's dinner table covered in platters of succulent roasted lamb, herbed ham, steaming piles of fresh potatoes, veggies, home baked bread and buckets of strong scalding tea. If Thomas Kincaid had painted Ireland, he could have easily started with Aunt Rita's house.

Just down the main road from my mother's ancestral home, lived my mother's other sister and my Aunt Kitty with her daughter Mary and dog Dinky. Aunt Kitty would have the dubious honor, and as it turned out, the Atlas like burden, of caring for my brother and me during the Bueller trip.

Aunt Kitty was by all accounts the black sheep of the Nolan sisters and definitely the party girl of the lot. I don't remember seeing an old photo of my Aunt Kitty that wasn't at a dance or, a party, and most of the photographs included a cigarette in one hand and a drink in the other. Strikingly beautiful in her youth, with shoulder length jet black hair, ruby lips, fairer than fair complexion she reminded me of Snow White. Full figured from the start, she grew a bit bustier with age, but her looks stayed with her mellowing gracefully all the way.

Aunt Kitty's place was really more of a townhouse or what the Irish call a semi-detached, meaning that several distinct homes occupied the same common building. Mr. Doyle lived next door and although he did not remind me of my grandfather, he did remind me of the type of man Hollywood has always portrayed should be my grandfather. He was kind and funny and built numerous toys for us in the small woodworking shop that occupied the back portion of his property.

The other next door neighbor was really not a neighbor at all but a small grocery reminiscent of the small town food market that was a part of every village in every country on every continent before it was decided that shopping in an aircraft hangar, with a push truck buying two weeks' worth of chemically preserved food was a better idea. We were in that little grocery store five, six or seven times a day when my Aunt decided she needed an onion,(yes, she bought them one at a time) a couple of potatoes, a pint of milk, or when we had five or ten pents in our pockets to buy a Cadbury bar.

I believe my aunt was married twice, or maybe it was more, I'm not sure. People would call her both Kitty Mellon and Kitty Thompson, depending, I suppose, on what stage in her life they met her. She was never married while we were kids and on the topic of marriage I cannot remember a positive comment from my aunt.

One thing for sure was that one of her husbands was a mechanic, as there was a cavernous automotive shop attached to her home and it made up the bulk of the property. My brother and I, along with cousins Jim and John (Rita's boys) spent endless hours exploring the garage, sitting in the driver's seats of several abandoned wrecks, spinning the steering wheels, working the clutch and stick shift and pretending we were Mario

Andretti racing for the checkered flag. I suppose it was this automotive angle that led Aunt Kitty to the only occupation I ever remember her having and her only visible means of support.

You see, Aunt Kitty drove a taxi. More succinctly, she owned and operated the most popular clandestine taxi service in south County Dublin. As it is in New York, London or any large city, operating a taxi is a very lucrative business. It is in large part lucrative because government licensing limits the competition. A Dublin taxi license even back then cost several thousands of pounds, if you could even find one. Taxi licenses were passed down from generation to generation, and if they were sold, went for many times more than their face value. Of course government licensing and regulation also drive up the cost of the taxi business and keep rates high resulting in essentially an additional tax on consumers.

Aunt Kitty disagreed with this heavy handed government approach and she was certainly not an advocate of higher taxes. Looking back at it now, I suppose my Aunt Kitty was the first real Libertarian I ever met. Maybe that is where I get my libertarian tendencies. Regardless, Kitty believed that the role of government in private enterprise should be strictly limited and taxes should remain low. Being more than just a philosophical advocate of free and unfettered markets, and committed to sparing as many of her fellow citizens from unnecessary taxation as possible, she bravely put her beliefs into practice and started her own unlicensed, unregulated taxi service.

Although obviously a courageous entrepreneur and champion of the little man, there was, nonetheless, no sense in openly tweaking the noses of the establishment. While we were living with my aunt that summer, we had standing instructions not to talk openly about the business, and to refer to customers as "friends". Also, if anybody from the County of Dublin Business Office, or police for that matter, came by, we were to tell them that Aunt Kitty was out of town for two weeks visiting a sick friend.

Aunt Kitty ended up giving "friends" rides all over county Dublin and even into the neighboring county Wicklow as her free market approach gave her an advantage over her more orthodox competition since very few taxi services could afford multi county licenses. We would end up accompanying Aunt Kitty on many of her trips meeting a wonderful collection of characters along the way, occasionally having to hide in bushes or behind buildings(great fun!) and participating in at least one low speed chase many years before O.J. Simpson had made such things popular.

As for the rest of the family, Uncle Jim lived up the Tanney road well off the main drag and was the unofficial town historian. He also started a small private bank, a savings and loan, and issued the first credit cards at a time when English usury laws were taking a punishing toll on the local populace. His house is still there today and the financial institutions live on in the form of a local organization called The Society, run on and off by various cousins. My Aunt Eileen has a flat in Dundrum, my Aunt Betty lives in the neighboring village of Sandyford, and assorted cousins, aunts and uncles all still live in and around Dundrum.

The Lads in Dublin
Transatlantic Journey

In the early Seventies, it was still a big deal to take a transatlantic flight and even more so to spend a summer in Europe. And if you were going to go, the 747 was the plane to go in. The plane had been out only a few years and its size and distinct shape made it unique in the aviation world. This was the first commercial jet with two passenger decks, the lower main passenger deck and the upper First Class deck that gave the aircraft its unique front "hump". The first time I saw the plane at Kennedy International Airport, I was awestruck. It was parked up close to the terminal attached to a jet way and you could see the entire aircraft through the huge picture windows. Even more awe inspiring was that I would be flying in this magnificent machine across the Atlantic Ocean, and because of Brian's negotiating abilities, I would be flying what today would be called Business Class.

Apparently there was a lot of work to be done before we ever boarded the plane to Ireland. As mentioned earlier, our traveling companions and benefactors were two spinster sisters from St. Cecelia's Parish. The sisters had come into a large sum of money through the death of a brother in the casket business. After the brother was laid to rest in one of his own products, the sisters inherited the business, which provided them a very comfortable living until, they too, became their own customers.

Quickly on the heels of their new found wealth, a trip to Ireland came to the top of their agenda. Somehow, and I really don't want to know exactly how it came about, Father Bueller became indispensable to the journey. So much so that the sisters never blinked when told that Brian and I were somehow essential to the success of this odyssey and they picked up all the expenses for our trip.

As I mentioned, much work needed to be done before we embarked on our trip. After checking in our baggage, our next objective, - after stopping off at an airport bar to deal with what was being described as a "desperate thirst", - was the Duty Free Shop.

The shop was brightly lit with row upon row upon row of every kind of alcoholic beverage you could imagine, glistening in clear, amber and emerald bottles. Cartons of cigarettes were stacked in huge pyramids that ran down the center of the shop and all types of chocolates, smoked salmon and other delicacies were scattered on various display tables on either side of the tobacco mountains. Our fellow travelers scurried amongst the cornucopia with sparkling eyes and gleefully mischievous faces. They seemed to be stuffing at random as many bottles, cartons and boxes as possible into large bags with rope handles emblazoned with the words DUTY FREE.

I was not familiar with the term "Duty-Free" and I asked FB what it meant. Father Bueller succinctly explained it to me.

It was here that I got one of my first lessons in how taxation worked. Now I had not learned this in over 6 years of formal religious instruction, but apparently Jesus abhorred taxes, going so far as to recruit a tax collector as a disciple to get him away from such an evil profession.

After Father Bueller's brief dissertation, it did seem that avoiding taxes was certainly the Lord's work, and the work was being done in spades at Kennedy International. At any rate, after the brief lesson on Christianity and taxes, Brian and I were given five bucks, told to leave our carry-on bags with Bueller and the sisters, and go and get some chocolates for the trip.

After returning with the chocolates, Bueller gave us our carry-on luggage and we headed for the departure gate. My bags, as well as Brian's, seemed to have gained considerable weight since last we had carried them. My comment to this effect was dismissed by FB who said "Nonsense lads. Things always seem heavier right before you fly." Somehow, that made sense at the time.

Now you have to remember that at this time airport security was not what it is today. The security was run by the airlines. It was paid for by the airlines. And in reality, they were probably more interested in not angering passengers than they were in stopping hijackers, which was the threat back then. Your carry-on bag was not routinely searched and they certainly didn't run you through a naked body scanner or put their hands down your pants looking for underwear bombs. Unless you were trying to get on the flight with a loaded .45, you were probably left mostly unmolested.

Nonetheless, trying to take more duty free booze from one country into another was still an offense that had a pretty hefty fine attached to it. As we approached the departure gate, Bueller got a little more serious and told Brian and me to stay close to him. However, dressed in clerical garb and using his native gift of the gab, (I believe FB not only kissed the Blarney Stone, he probably chipped off a piece and carried it around in his pocket), Father Bueller got us through the departure gate and, unbeknownst to me at the time, I smuggled 4 quarts of Jameson's Irish Whiskey and eight hundred Pall Mall cigarettes across International lines. I was a mule long before I had any idea what the term actually meant.

The flight across the Atlantic was an exciting adventure. We were allowed all the soda we could drink and there was a never ending supply of chips, pretzels, candy and other snacks. About halfway through the journey, I watched with amazement as a screen descended from the ceiling of the cabin and it was announced that a movie would be shown.

Again, you have to remember, this was years before home VCRs came out, before cable television, and in my house, we still had a black and white TV. Not that we didn't have some advanced technology. My father did have one of the first voice activated television remote controls. Actually he had two remote controls. They were called Kevin and Brian. When my Dad was watching TV, one of us was always required to be in the room. Periodically he would shout out, "Kevin, channel ten", or "Brian, channel thirteen" and we would have to pop up and twist the dial to the designated station. Thank God there were only four channels.

So seeing a movie anywhere except a movie theatre was pretty big stuff. Our seats were also close to the front, next to the spiral staircase that leads to first class. Now as I mentioned, Bueller and the spinsters had first class tickets and, although we were clearly told that nobody but First Class was allowed up the stairs, we decided we had to have a look.

We waited until the stewardesses were serving dinner and when both were in the galley together, first Brian, and then I, quickly corkscrewed up the stairs. It was surreal. At the top of the stairs, keeping ourselves well below the level of the upper deck, we could see the whole setup in First Class. There was a bar, tables, and then rows of chairs that looked like big Lazy Boy Recliners. It was hard to believe we were in an airplane traveling hundreds of miles an hour across a vast ocean. Bueller was at the bar; drink in one hand, Pall Mall in the other. (Smoking was not only allowed on flights, the cigarettes were complementary in First Class. Free also was all the booze you could drink. Bueller was in Heaven.) His hands were gesturing excitedly, tiny waves of Jameson's breaking the rim of the glass and crashing on the bar below as he regaled several passengers with some intriguing tale that, judging by the grins on the faces of his fellow First Classers, was going over magnificently.

One of the spinsters was asleep by a window seat. A drink still precariously held in her lap at a dangerous angle indicated that perhaps her current nap may not have been completely planned. The other spinster was in the middle of the lounge area getting what appeared to be a lesson in an Irish jig. Unfortunately, every time she tried to lift one leg off the ground, the old darling became unsteady and started to fall over. A popular commercial jingle at the time for a child's toy popped in my head, "Weebles wobble but they don't fall down…" They appeared to be having a great time.

We decided that we would go up and join them and see if Father Bueller could use his silver tongue to get us permission to stay for a while. It wasn't to be. Just as we decided to further ascend the staircase, I felt a large cold hand grip the back of my neck. It was the stewardess who told us in the first place that we were not allowed up there, and we were summarily escorted back to our lower class seats.

Nonetheless, our seats were hardly steerage, and we enjoyed wonderful meals, drinks and movies until we landed on the Emerald Isle, putting down at Shannon Airport.

The Old Sod

Shannon Airport is located in County Clare right
on the coast, tucked just a few miles upstream of
the Atlantic on the famed Shannon River.
Limerick, the renowned Irish city that lent its name
to the more often than not risqué poetic device, is a
short fifteen minute drive east.

In the Seventies, there were no direct flights from
the US to Dublin. All flights had to stop in
Shannon. Originally this was out of necessity
since Shannon was the most western airport in all
of Europe and thus the closest geographically to
America. The airport sprung up as a result of the
first planes to cross the Atlantic, flying boats, that
would land in the Shannon River and then cruise
upstream to a series of docks that are now the
airport. Later, when conventional aircraft began
making the transatlantic run, fuel limitations were
an issue and Shannon airport became an important
refueling stop for all aircraft bound for Europe
from America.

However, now with the 747, fuel was not an issue,
as this aircraft was fully capable of going non-stop

from America to Dublin, not to mention London, Paris or Rome, if it was so desired.

This was a problem at Shannon Airport as they had grown nicely comfortable with the revenue that was a result of all the transatlantic refueling stops. Thanks to a strong Irish Lobby in Washington, a stopover rule was put in place requiring US planes to land in Shannon before continuing on to their final destination. Even though the ticket on the flight said Dublin, most passengers to Ireland from New York in the early Seventies wound up beginning their Irish odyssey on the desolate plains of the Western Irish coast. So more out of politics than necessity, we found ourselves at Shannon.

Aircraft travel then was a little more civilized than it is today. Unlike modern jet travel where upon landing the passengers immediately jump up and start scurrying through the overheads in their haste to get out of this flying tube, the passengers then were in no rush to disembark. As a matter of fact, there was no practical reason to rush to the overheads. Although modern jet ways that attached the aircraft directly to the terminal were in use, Shannon was not exactly at the cutting edge of modern passenger aircraft technology. As a matter of fact, a quick glance through the starboard windows of our airplane indicated that we were still a good five hundred yards from the terminal building.

Brian and I were still, quite frankly, happy to be comfortably ensconced in our seats, still sucking down Cokes and also, following Father Bueller's pre-flight instructions, grabbing as many loose small bottles of booze we could find to stick into our carry-on.

We had also been given some very strange instructions by our mother to grab all the air sickness bags we could find on the flight and give them to our Aunt Kitty when we arrived in Dublin. We had no idea what the reason was for this odd directive, but nonetheless, we carried it out.

All of a sudden, the passenger compartment broke out with a flurry of activity. Like a school of fish all suddenly breaking direction at the same time, the passengers arose and went for the overheads with purpose. I glanced out the window to see two toy like looking vehicles heading for our mammoth plane. One was clearly a bus and the other was an odd looking truck that when it finally turned its profile toward the plane, was supporting a huge staircase.

There was still no sign of Bueller or the spinsters from the upper deck, but we took the flurry of activity around us as a sign that maybe we too should get ready to disembark.

A moment or two later, two stewardesses and a very serious looking man who had just descended from the spiral staircase, were wrestling the door of the plane open just to our left. First pulling some levers, and then wrestling the door first inward toward the plane and then out and to the side, this team opened the front door of the plane and a rush of cold, wet air invaded our happy domain. Instructions were issued and it became obvious that those of us in the front of the plane were expected to start exiting as soon as possible. There was still no sign of Bueller, but we figured we should obey the directions being given by these uniformed individuals, so Brian and I grabbed our gear and headed for the door.

Disembarking from an airplane back then was also much more of an adventure than it is today. Instead of passing through the aircraft door into a corridor that is not much different from the cabin environment you just left, you stepped out the door to be on a platform, supported by stairs that were on the back of a truck; a truck that didn't look much different from the pickup truck my friend Michael's Dad had back home.

Now on a 747, when you stepped out from the plane, you were stepping out to a height of about fifty feet or almost a four story building. From the tarmac of the Shannon airport, the desolate flat plains of western Ireland spread out for miles. The

Airport was unimpressive, not the spectacular buildings that made up JFK from where we had departed. The view was beautiful though. Once you glanced past the terminal building and the few functional, ancillary structures that made up Shannon airport, you could see the picturesque landscape of Irish countryside, a patchwork of small fields of green, each one laying its own claim to the legendary forty shades known in song and story. Although we were obviously not yet in Dublin, it was exciting to be in Ireland.

My brother and I descended the stairways of the truck, both of us burdened by huge carry- on bags. It became obvious that not only did carry- on luggage seem heavier before you flew, the phenomenon apparently extended until you were actually off the aircraft.

At the bottom of the stairways truck, we stepped to the side hoping that Father Bueller and the spinsters, like luggage on an airport carousel, would eventually appear.

A tall gentleman in green trousers, white shirt and wearing an official looking hat, turned to us to ask us the whereabouts of our parents. Deciding in mental unison that neither one of us wanted to explain to this gentleman that our parents were a priest and two drunken old ladies, we just pointed to the top of stairs and laughed.

At that moment, at the top of the stairs, appeared the two drunken old ladies. Father Bueller was directly behind them, but obscured by the spinsters, both of which had their hands raised in gladiatorial triumph declaring, "Yes, finally, were here in Dublin! Oh, isn't it gorgeous? What a magnificent city"

Now, I understand that these two old darlings had never been to Dublin, or any place else in Ireland for that matter. And yes, their ticket was a ticket to Dublin. But to mistake this Godforsaken place for a thriving metropolis of nearly a million souls was something of a stretch. Just to the north of this desolate piece of land lay the plains of Connaught. During Lord Cromwell's conquest of the island in the seventeenth century, he would famously reply, in response to a question of what would happen to anyone who defied English rule, "They may go to Hell or to Connaught." To Lord Cromwell, they were one fate in the same.

Well, the old gals descended the stairs and when they reached the bottom, they dropped to their knees and kissed the ground celebrating their arrival on the old sod, despite the fact that what they were kissing was actually german asphalt. Bueller, not normally one to be embarrassed regardless of the situation, sidestepped the sisters, grabbed both of us by the arm and shoved us on to the bus. This was, after all, his home county.   As I made my way up the several steps of the bus, I heard the man in the green trousers and white shirt, in a voice with only slightly disguised disgust, remark, "Americans".

The bus transported us to the terminal building where a huge sign over the entrance greeted us with "Welcome to Ireland, please set your clocks back two hundred years". We quickly collected our luggage and this time through customs on the Irish side, Father Bueller had us stay back as he took a more proactive approach toward gaining access to the country.

We sat atop a huge pile of luggage and listened to the two old spinsters chatter on about being "home", the land of their ancestors and wondering if Glocca Morra was nearby and if they would see any leprechauns. Glocca Morra? That was from the fantasy film "Finians Rainbow" for crying out loud. And Leprechauns? Really? Leprechauns? I don't think I really even need to comment on that.

As all this was going on, I could see Bueller standing at the customs desk having an animated chat with the fellow behind the counter. He was laughing and gesturing and appearing much like he did at the bar in the plane sans the booze and the butts.

It wasn't long before FB was gesturing excitedly for us to come forward and the man behind the counter opened a small side door behind his desk and all of us were ushered through. Just out of earshot, the official gave Father Bueller a series of verbal instructions, FB handed the gentleman a bottle of Jameson's and a carton of Pall Malls, shook his hand and we were on our way. The hall way led to a door which led to the parking lot and suddenly we were out of Shannon Airport.

In the parking lot, Father Bueller quickly glanced around, immediately found what he wanted, and moved with purpose. "There it is, Hertz. Let's go everyone; I want to get out of here as quickly as possible."

At the Hertz counter, it appeared Father Bueller was disappointed in the selection of cars available. They must have been fresh out of POS Chevy Novas and he had to settle for something else. As it turned out, that something else was a French built Renault. His parting comment at the check-out desk drew raucous laughter from the attendants. It would be years later before I would appreciate his remark that he would take the car, but certainly hoped it would not immediately give up at the first sign of trouble.

Leaving the airport, FB instinctively started driving on the right side of the road. An oncoming produce truck clued him in that, oh yea, this was Ireland and maybe I should be on the other side of the highway. Upon leaving the airport, we were immediately lost.

Now you have to understand that getting directions in Ireland is different than getting directions in almost any other part of the world. There is a protocol. There is a procedure, and there are certain rules. You don't think those famous signposts with arrows going in all directions to all manner of destination just happened by accident do you?

This direction asking and answering protocol is deeply steeped in Irish culture. There are several specific steps in the exchange, and YOU MUST NOT SKIP ANY STEPS. This will not only aid you in getting directions when you need them, it will serve you well later with all the Irish you may encounter.

First some insight into the psyche of the Irish. Do not try to get right to the point of any matter, with any Irishman, anywhere, as much as you may be tempted to do so. The Irishman will not go there naturally nor will he be coerced. Whether it's giving directions or arguing politics, the Irishman will *eventually* get to the point, but it is going to be in a roundabout way. As a matter of fact, this roundaboutness is so deeply ingrained in the Irish culture that the Irish roads do not even meet at direct right angles to each other. The roads actually intersect *into roundabouts,* where lost American tourists can be found any time of day or night, anytime of the year, endlessly driving in circles futilely trying to read signposts in Gaelic and frozen with fear that they may suddenly exit in the wrong direction and be lost forever.

So just that you know, The Steps are: Inquisition for directions, forlorn response laced with hopelessness or disgust, second request for help, notification of the inability to travel from the current location to the desired location, third desperate request for help, directions detailing the path not to take, a final pitiful plea for assistance, and finally, directions using landmarks that only would be known to someone native from the area who certainly wouldn't need directions in the first place. A typical exchange would go something like this:

LOST: "Excuse me sir, do you know the way to Dublin?" IRISH: "Dublin? Jaysus, Mary and Joseph, why would you ever want to go to that place?" LOST: "Ugh, well we're visiting some relatives, my aunt actually, and ughm, well, at any rate, do you know which road I want to take?" IRISH: "A road you'll be wanting is it? Well there's no road to Dublin from here. Who've you been talking to who's after telling you this is the Dublin road? Someone's been messing with you man." LOST: "Oh, well, ugh no, actually, nobody told me that this was the road to Dublin, you see…" IRISH: "Well if nobody told you this was the road to Dublin, what are you doing here? Look here, I'm a busy man, I've no time for your games." LOST: "Please, would you just tell me how to get to Dublin?" IRISH: "Well, if you keep going on this road you'll come to Murphy's pub. The road will veer off to the left and then look for the cemetery. Now just before you're able to see the cemetery, the road veers again but this time to the right. After about a mile, you'll come to a fork in the road." LOST: "Well then, which way should I go for Dublin, left or right?" IRISH: "For Dublin? Jaysus, neither one. One road goes to Kerry and the other to Cork. No, if you want to go to Dublin stay off that road altogether, it'll do you no good at all." LOST: "Look, please, for the love of God, can you tell me how to get to Dublin?" IRISH: "Well of course I can. Sure haven't I lived here all of my life? What kind of an eejit would I be if I couldn't tell you how to get to Dublin? Now, simply drive up the road here until you get to the new Flannigan farm, not the elder Flannigan, but his boy Paddy, you know the one that went off to that fancy school in England….."

And so it would go. Fortunately, we had a native from Clare at the tiller, fully versed in Irish direction giving. Soon we were on the motorway to Dublin.

In pre European Union Ireland, the term "motorway" could be a bit misleading. In most countries, the term "motorway" means a road designed for the use of motorized vehicles. Not necessarily so in Ireland. In Ireland the designation "motorway" more often than not does not mean that the road was designed for motor vehicles, just that you are allowed to drive your motor vehicle on it. For the most part, many of the roads have been little improved for use by cars and trucks since first constructed for cart and donkey.

The roads can often be no more than what we would consider a narrow lane and are typically lined on both sides with short dry stone walls. These walls, built without the aid of any mortar, have stood for hundreds of years and line all the roads and separate the various fields giving form to the famous patchwork of green that is visible from altitude.

Often there appears to be absolutely no reason as to why some of these walls were built as the serve neither to keep anything in or anyone out. As the story goes, apparently this terrain was so rocky that in the process of clearing the fields for planting and grazing, so many rocks started accumulating that the only logical thing to do was to start stacking them up and spreading them out. The endeavor to dispose of the stone became an enterprise unto itself and today there are thousands of miles of these walls spread across the length and breadth of the island.

However, a few short miles of driving on these roads finds most travelers wishing the locals had invested more time in road construction and less in wall building. Unless the road carries the specific designation "dual carriageway", be prepared to pull off to one side if you happen to encounter traffic coming in the opposite direction.

While driving these roads a relentless voice in the back of your head keeps saying, "surely this can't be the road to Dublin. We must have taken a wrong turn." Indeed you keep expecting to turn a corner and come face to face with a large Manor House because surely the "road" that you were on must be a long driveway and not the main thoroughfare between an International Airport and a National Capital. Actually a wrong turn may put you on the winding drive to an old country manor house or castle and indeed you may not realize you had veered off the main drag until you came face to face with the front gates of the estate.

The trip from Shannon to Dublin is about one hundred and twenty five miles. The Renault performed flawlessly, much to Father Bueller's surprise, and we covered the journey in a mere six hours. Upon arrival at Aunt Kitty's house everyone congratulated each other that we had made "good time".

As we pulled up in front of my Aunt Kitty's place, directions were issued on disembarking from the journey. "Okay lads, go knock on the front door and tell your Auntie that you're here, I'll get the bags out", and my brother and I obediently bolted for the massive front door of the old Georgian townhouse, lifted the enormous lion's head that comprised the door's brass knocker and began banging away. In no time, Aunt Kitty was at the door with daughter Mary and dog Dinky and we were greeted as prodigal sons with big hugs and sloppy old lady kisses, smiles and further instructions on what to do with our luggage.

Eager to get settled and then of course into the first mischief we could find, we bolted back to the car to find our suitcases out of the trunk(boot) and our carry-on bags set on top. "Okay, lads grab your carry-on bags, and I'll take in the suitcases" came the directions from FB which we quickly followed, excited to see what our digs for the summer would look like.

Upon picking up our carry-on bags and heading for the door, I felt a sense of profound amazement.

Although I still did not completely understand this strange phenomenon, it was undoubtedly true. Our bags were now much lighter, significantly lighter than when we were flying just as Father Bueller had said. It was interesting, and I made a mental note to ask Father Bueller more about this later, but right now the excitement of this new adventure had taken center stage and we were looking forward to whatever was coming next no matter what it was.

Aunt Kitty, Father Bueller and the two old ladies were busy introducing themselves, exchanging greetings from my mother and details of the trip. All agreed that modern jet travel was a marvel, the roads were desperate, and a national scandal, but the scenery was lovely and, all an all, a grand journey.

Now I understand that in Arab Culture there is a custom that if a visitor comes to your house and compliments one of your belongings, the host must offer to give that item to the guest. The custom also dictates that the guest must refuse the gift. The host must again offer the item to the guest and again it must be refused. Finally the host must insist that the guest take the item in question and again, the guest must firmly refuse. On the third refusal, the terms of the custom are satisfied, the participants released, and host and guest may continue on with their pleasantries.

In Ireland there is a similar custom, but it does not revolve around a possession of the host as such, but rather with tea, and Father Bueller, Aunt Kitty and the old ladies were now just beginning to engage in the Irish Tea Exchange.

You see, when you show up at an Irish home, whether as family member, a guest or a complete stranger, the host must offer you tea. The tea must first be refused. It must be offered again and refused again. Now here, the Irish Tea Exchange exhibits a bit more flexibility than the Arab custom. After a second refusal, a third offer must be made but after that, the participants are free to take the exchange in any number of directions, perhaps a beer, or maybe whisky, a lite bite to eat or maybe just a sandwich. The point is, the host must get the guest to accept something or risk eternal damnation and social ridicule. I've actually gone to the house of an Irish friend of ours with my mother and sat and watched as she was offered tea three times, a glass of wine, a cold drink and a sandwich and she refused all. Then, at a visit to a second Irish friend, when the name of the first Irish friend was brought up, my mother would say, "Oh yes, we were at Mary's the other day, and you know I sat there for twenty minutes and never even got a cup of tea", truly incredible!

At any rate, FB, Aunt Kitty and Old Ladies had concluded the Exchange and tea had been agreed upon. As the adults went into the house and headed for the sitting room, Mary offered to bring us upstairs and show us our room. Before heading up the stairs, Mary stopped and asked us, "Oh lads, do you have the bags?" Both Brian and I looked back at Mary somewhat confused as indeed we had two large suitcases and two large carry-ons sitting on the floor next to us. We glanced down at the luggage and then back up at Mary. We obviously "had the bags." "No, No, No, THE BAGS. Didn't your mum tell you to grab all the air sickness bags you could find before getting off the plane at Shannon?" Now it clicked. "Oh yea, we have them right here, we grabbed all we could." I said as we both dug through our carry on and delivered the rectangular wax lined receptacles to our cousin. Curiosity got the better of me. "Mary, what do you plan to do with all these bags? I asked. "Never mind, but they're very important", she replied. "Thanks for getting them." Then she shoved the bags into a drawer in the hall table and showed us up the stairs.

By the time we had finished unpacking, tea was done, and we said our goodbyes to Bueller and the old ladies and our Irish adventure had begun. Arrangements had been made that Father Bueller would return in three months' time to "collect the lads" and take us back to America. That sounded

155

simple at the time, but would end up being an entire adventure in itself.

Into the City

Twenty minutes after arriving at our Aunt Kitty's, my brother and I were bored out of our minds. Fortunately, just at that moment, my cousins Jim and John (Rita's boys) arrived at the doorstep looking to meet their American cousins. My Aunt was well relieved, as I think she realized twenty minutes into this deal that she had three more months with us, and how in God's name was she going to keep us busy and out of her way. She welcomed the boys in with great enthusiasm, much to Jim's surprise, and grabbed her carpetbagger sized purse off the hall table. "Jim, here's five pounds. I want you to take Kevin and Brian into Dublin and show them the city center. There should be plenty there for something to eat and some sweets." Both Jim and John's eyes opened wide with shock. It struck me that I don't think either one of them was accustomed to getting five pound notes from their Auntie and told to go into town on their own and load up on sweets and junk food. No questions were asked and we were told to follow the boys as we were given something of

156

a bums rush out the front door and we were on our way, walking up the Dundrum road to catch a 48A bus into the city.

The bus stop was actually located in front of Uncle Tom's cabin, which was directly in front of Jim and John's house. Jim shouted out, "Let's stop in Uncle Tom's and see my Da".

Uncle Matt was of course Aunt Rita's husband, father to Jim, John and Paula, and a bit of a mystery to me all my life. He was from county Kerry so he carried the tag of "Kerryman" all his days. For some reason, the people from Kerry were the butt of a certain genre of jokes known as Kerryman jokes. The jokes revolved around the stupidity of people from Kerry and were almost identical to the Polock jokes we liked to tell when we were kids. You know the jokes. "How many Kerryman does it take to screw in a light bulb?" "Three, one to hold the bulb and two to spin the chair." "A Kerryman put in his will that he wanted to be buried at sea and three of his friends drown digging the grave." Well, you get the idea.

Matt was far from stupid and was the kindest soul I know. True to his Irish heritage, he was passionate about drink and had a love affair with cigarettes that would make Bogart and Bacall look like a passing acquaintance. He truly smoked them and cared not what the brand was, filter, no filter, regular, menthol it didn't matter. If it was a cigarette, Matt embraced it. Like an illicit lover, he extracted all the pleasure that it had to offer and would suck the very essence from it before crushing it out and looking for his next mistress.

That next mistress could be another cigarette or a pint of Guinness Stout for he was as passionate about the drink as the fag he smoked with it. Matt knew all the pubs that served the best pint and was a wonderful resource for making sure that if you were going out for the night in Dublin, you didn't make the dreaded mistake of providing custom to a public house that served an inferior product.

Matt knew how to order the drink saying simply, "pint please", as Guinness was the default setting for any decent barman or publican in the country. He would watch it being poured with all the enthusiasm and excitement of a new father in the delivery room. First half was poured and then the drink was left on its own, however still providing entertainment for its eventual owner as you sat and watched the black creamy liquid cascade down the glass. Soon enough, the barman would return to finish the process, first tipping the glass forward then back, the tap pushed back, then forth and then back again, until a perfect creamy white head mushroomed just over the rim of the glass, sitting on top of a solid ebony body. The Blonde in the Black Dress.

We found Matt in the bar section of Uncle Tom's. Irish pubs, at least the traditional ones, always had two distinct sections, the bar and the lounge. Each section had its own separate entrance and loos (restrooms) and functioned independently, even though they were almost always connected, and patrons of either section could easily access both sides, or not.

You see, in a more genteel era not that long ago, a respectable woman would never go into a pub. However, it was completely acceptable to go into a lounge and drink to your heart's content. There was also the question of families. A "pub" of course is a public house, and many people did treat it as an extension of their home. Of course a house wouldn't be a home without kids, so the lounge side was also the family side. If Da wanted to go for a drinking session, it would be considered bad form to bring the kids into the bar area, but put them on the other side of the pub, give them a soda and a bag of chips and Dad could go and get completely legless with his mates and no foul called. Ma could come along as well and plow through countless half pints of her favorite beverage (a woman would never order or drink a pint in public. Even if she was planning to put away a dozen or so drinks, she would do it in half pints only). The wife could catch up with the local gossip, the kids stayed entertained playing with the other neighbor kids, and you could even have dinner if by chance you got overserved.

Now I know what you're thinking, and you're right. In today's age, Child Protective Services would probably break down the door and haul off parents that brought their kids to a bar, got hammered and allowed the children to run around half wild with a bunch of other kids who had been brought to a bar by their parents while they got half crocked. However in the Ireland of forty years ago, the neighborhoods were still quite tight, everyone knew whose kids were whose and parents were not at all shy about disciplining any child, regardless of ownership. The kids knew this too and it kept them in line for they never knew who might be watching and at any time any adult could come along and box their ears and haul them off to their parents for further discipline. Believe it or not, it was actually quite a family friendly affair.

As I said, we found Matt in the bar section of Uncle Tom's completely absorbed in the current edition of the racing form. I never knew Matt to actually have a job in the traditional get up in the morning, trudge off somewhere with a lunch pail, come back at night and then do it all over again, sense of the word. That doesn't mean he didn't work hard. Matt was all business when it came to the horses and he did his homework. He read the racing forms, talked with the jockeys, watched the races and knew some of the owners. Matt did his due diligence and he was a respected authority on horse flesh. He strategically positioned himself at Uncle Tom's which happened to be just across the street from Paddy Power book makers. Off Track Betting is legal all across Ireland, and Paddy Power is a chain of retail betting shops.

Matt would listen to the various races with a portable AM/FM radio, a white wire constantly dangling from his ear. At just the right moment, so as not to tip off too many other bettors and change the odds, Matt could jump up from his barstool, rush across the street and place a strategic bet just seconds before the window closed. Matt's office was perfect. What do they say about real estate? Location, location, location.

We walked into the pub with Jim and John. We were greeted with "Hello lads, are you well?" as Matt looked up from his paper. "Jaysus, I see you have Brian and Kevin with you. Hello lads, are you just in from America". We informed our Uncle that yes indeed we were just in from America and were heading into Dublin. "Dublin is it? Augh, well that's grand, you're wasting no time then. Jim, bring them home with you tonight for your suppers. I'll let your Ma know and I'll sort it out with Kitty." Looking out the window he said, "Oh right, here's your bus now lads" and then bending down to whisper into Jim's ear he said, "Jim, before you go, run across to Paddy's and put this down on Gin Mill in the Fifth at Astor", and he slipped a five pound note into my cousin's hand.

We rushed out to catch our bus and Jim ran across the street to place the bet. Matt must have been losing his clandestine touch as five guys in the bar followed Jim across the street to the bookie.

The buses were huge monsters to someone who came from a suburban area with no mass transit. They were Kelly green, double decked leviathans, their sides emblazoned with cheerful faces encouraging all who they passed to "Drink Guinness for Strength" or "Smoke John Player for True Tobacco Satisfaction". They roared along the narrow Dublin streets dominating and intimidating the tiny Fiats, Renaults, Minis and other motorized roller skates the Irish used for cars. I would actually cringe as these green goliaths would zip in and out of traffic with incredible agility averting disaster by centimeters and seemingly constantly on the verge of catastrophe.

We hopped on the 48A and raced up the spiral staircase of the Kelly green double decker so we could get a seat with a view. Although fully automated now with PassCards and electronic fare devices, in the early Seventies, the busses still had conductors. There were three entrances on those old buses. There was the front, where the driver sat, a bi-fold door in the middle, and then an open section on the end of the bus where there was a pole to grab on to.

The back was by far the best place to get on the bus as you could run and catch a moving bus, jumping on the back and grabbing the pole before the big green beast got up too much steam. As kids, this was by far our most favored method of engaging public transportation, going so far as to wait for a standing bus to pull away before we got on, rather than board in the more conventional manner. This also helped us avoid conductors.

The conductors all looked like Ralph Kramden, with the nondescript uniform, hat pushed back on their heads, the pot belly and upon that belly they balanced a small barrel like device, with a crank handle on one end and supported by a neck strap.

 The job of the conductor was to walk the aisle of the bus after everyone got on, inquire as to their destination, collect the fare, and then turn the handle on the barrel to produce a receipt for the passenger.

Our job was to avoid the conductor as long as possible. You see, the way we figured it, every shilling that we didn't have to pay for bus fare, we could convert into sweets and other things we really wanted and hadn't yet figured out how not to pay for. We were young and agile, the conductor old and slow. The advantage was clearly in our court.

Conductors always went upstairs last so by heading to the upper deck, you could ride for blocks before ever having to deal with the Man. If you were good, and we were, when the conductor ascended to the upper deck, you could slip back down to the lower deck again extending your free travel time. Sometimes this strategy was enough to get you all the way to your destination. Other times, the open back ends of these great behemoths made just as convenient an escape point as an entry point and during that summer we became quite adept at jumping off a moving bus while maintaining our composure.

This bus would take us right into the City Centre, "An Lar" in Irish, and drop us along Nassau Street that runs along the south side of Trinity College.

We spent our first full day with my cousins in Dublin. The river Liffey divides Dublin North and South and two canals, the Grand on the south side and the Royal on the north side form the boundaries of what's considered the City Centre.

From the bus stop, we walked Grafton St., a wonderful wide, all pedestrian avenue filled with every manner of shops, restaurants and pubs. We strolled Steven's Green throwing stones at the pigeons, much to the disgust of the locals, and then crossed to the North Side of the Liffey via the Ha'penny Bridge.

The Ha'penny Bridge is an all cast iron bridge that was built in the early 19th century to replace the aging ferries that would shuttle pedestrians back and forth across the Liffey. The bridge was built with private money by the ferry company, and to compensate them they were allowed to charge a half penny (Ha'penny) to cross. The toll has since been suspended, but the name endures. Once on the North side, we visited the GPO (General Post Office) on O'Connell St. where Cousin Jim gave me one of my first lessons in Irish history.

They say that one of the first things a young Irish school boy learns is how to form a simple declarative sentence without using the word "Fuck". The second thing that same young schoolboy learns is all about the 1916 Easter Uprising, the Heroes, and the central role of the GPO.

For centuries, Ireland had been under an iron fisted British rule. On Easter Monday, 1916 James Connolly commanding the Irish Citizen army seized the GPO, and several other strategic sites in and around Dublin, and proclaimed the Irish Republic and Independence from Britain. The GPO became the headquarters of the Irish uprising and fighting ensued for seven days. Losses were heavy on both sides, but the arrival of British reinforcements and heavy guns, including a British gunboat the *Helga* which sailed up and down the Liffey shelling Irish positions, spelled doom for the Rebels and they surrendered unconditionally.

It can be argued though that the Rebellion was not a failure. Two years later Republicans, running on a platform of Irish independence secured seventy three of the one hundred and five Irish seats in the British parliament and the outrage over the execution of the Rebel leaders led directly to the Irish War of Independence in 1919.

Our history lesson concluded, Jim decided that our next stop should be the Guinness Brewery.

Located at St. James Gate in an area of Dublin known as "The Liberties", the Guinness brewery was at one time the largest brewery in the world. Our family had an indirect connection with the brewery as our Aunt Rosie's family worked for the

Guinness family for generations and her family lived on the Guinness estate for many, many years.

I say "her" family, as her family was not my family. Aunt Rosie was not really an aunt, but just one of those close family friends who was around all the time so you called her Aunt Rosie. Her brothers, her father, her grandfather and great grandfather all worked for the behemoth brewer.

In those days, not really so long ago, Guinness was a true company town. Many of the employees lived on the Guinness estate, worked at the brewery and socialized almost exclusively with their fellow Guinness workers.

By trade, Rosie's family were coopers, that is, they made barrels, in this case barrels for Guinness. Long before the shiny silver containers we now call kegs were produced, beer was packaged in wooden barrels made up of individual narrow slats of wood held tightly together by metal hoops. Hoops of iron, and later steel, were heated white hot in blacksmith furnaces and then slipped over the wooden barrel components. As the metal cooled and shrank it forced the wood slats together in a waterproof seal.

This occupation kept several generations of Aunt Rosie's family busy constructing the millions of barrels necessary to ship Guinness Stout around the world. It was considered very fortunate indeed to have a family position with Guinness. It provided job security, which was an incredible blessing in a country that, even in "good" times would run a twenty to twenty-five percent unemployment rate. You were treated with prestige and respect in the community as you were someone who had an inside track to get family members and friends a coveted Guinness job when they came up. But one of the most prized benefits was completely unknown to the company, and management was completely oblivious to it for many years.

You see, the St. James Gate home of Guinness covered some sixty or so acres and the buildings that housed the vats for the final aging of the Guinness and the buildings that housed where the stout would be kegged and then later bottled could be hundreds of yards apart. The solution to this problem was a series of pipes that ran from the brewing facilities to the kegging facilities. This pipe system kept a steady flow of Guinness from the vats to the kegging facilities and this kept a steady flow of stout to the people of Ireland and the world.

Well, there really shouldn't be any more to the story of the pipes than that. I mean, they were just another piece of infrastructure on a vast campus of industrial production. But you have to understand

168

something. You see, if the Guinness was being piped into one building from another, then there had to be someone, an Irish man, at the receiving end of the piping who was operating a valve that controlled millions of gallons of beautiful, creamy, Guinness Stout. It wouldn't take long for that same Irish man to figure out that a pipe was carrying the Guinness to him and that meant that underground there was millions of gallons of Guinness flowing like...like...like water, yes water. And if it was like water, sure then that was a gift from our Lord and free to all who availed themselves of it. I mean to an Irish man, the logic of it would have been undeniable.

Of course that is just what they did. It wasn't too long before a contingent of the coopers decided to do a safety check on the pipes. From that point on, they had their own personal brewery. At first they took down hammers and nails and a bucket. They would bang a nail into the iron pipe, pull it out, fill their bucket and then put the nail back. Eventually, all the coopers had their own "nail" like today's brew clubs where every member has his own mug. Each man would go down every night after work, fill up their lunch pails with Guinness and head for home. There is even an exhibit to this day in the Guinness museum showing a section of the pipe with all the nails in it. It looks like an iron porcupine. Of course it wasn't long before some particularly thirsty employees got greedy and installed a T-joint in the pipe.

Now you would think that eventually there would be a discrepancy between what was shipped from the vat house and what was kegged at the keg house, and I'm sure there was. But perhaps like any municipal water system today, a certain amount of loss was considered normal and no real cause for alarm. Apparently what raised the alarm for the company was the absenteeism. Work no shows began to soar and that threatened production more than any loss of Guinness in the pipes. It was in the course of investigating the sudden and virulent outbreak of the Irish flu that the clandestine pilferage of porter was uncovered.

From the brewery we hiked back to Nassau St. and the bus stop. A 48A brought us back to Dundrum, our first day in Dublin finished.

Mr. Kipaliti

Our days in Dublin passed quickly spent with my cousins Jim and John walking the streets of Dundrum, playing soccer in the vacant field across from my Aunt Kitty's and tormenting my cousin Mary.

Mary would have been in her early twenties and was a true Irish beauty, taking after her mother, my Aunt Kitty. Mary was preoccupied with all the things a young woman would be interested in, pop music, the latest fashions, dance clubs and boys. The last thing she wanted was two obnoxious American brats hanging around the house for the summer, and for good reason, as we made her life miserable.

She was at the time dating a young man named Bobby Byrnes, who would eventually become her husband. However, Mary's looks and bubbly

171

personality dictated that Bobby would not be the only suitor to visit the house. There was another chap Brian, a fellow named Tom (probably a Dick and a Harry too, I'm not sure) and several others that we saw only once. We knew though that Bobby was her favorite. Therefore, he was our target.

When Bobby would come to the house and Mary was out, we would answer the door and explain to Bobby that Brian, or Tom or whomever, had come by earlier and Mary had gone out with them (although she hadn't) and that she would be back very late as she was at a fancy restaurant and would be going clubbing after that. When Bobby called on the phone we would answer and tell him to hold on while we went to find Mary and then would leave the phone off the hook and never tell Mary. We stuffed a potato up the exhaust of his car when he came by for a big date, disabling the car and the date. We called and cancelled reservations while they were on their way to dinner, told my Aunt Kitty that the police had been by looking for Bobby, planted a dirty magazine in the pocket of Bobby's jacket while it was hanging on the hall coat rack so my Aunt could easily spot it, and generally acted like complete little shits. I'm not even sure exactly why we did it, because we actually liked Bobby. I guess we were just bored. Bobby, however, did get his revenge.

One evening, when Aunt Kitty was away, Bobby came by to pick up Mary for the evening. We were alone in the house and we stood with Bobby in the hallway as he waited for Mary to get ready. Bobby was unusually friendly and we chatted away with him as he showed a surprising interest in how our holiday was going and what we were doing. Now Bobby knew that house probably better than we did and when Mary shouted down the stairs that she would be down in a sec, Bobby turned to us and said, "Lads, we're going to need an umbrella tonight. I know there is a good one in the basement, in the closet at the bottom of the stairs. Would you go down and get it?" Well, that was a part of the house we hadn't been in yet so we enthusiastically responded that we would fetch the rain gear. Who knew what else we may find down there. Brian and I opened the door in the hallway and descended the steep wooden stairs that led to the cold, damp and smelly basement. At the base of the stairs, just as Bobby had promised, was a door that looked like the closet. We opened the door and stepped into the small, dank smelling, pitch black room. We searched for a light switch without success. Just as we were about to turn to yell up to Bobby that we couldn't see a thing, the door slammed shut. We heard a gleeful, richly satisfied laugh come from outside the door and Bobby said, "So long lads, we're off to fish and chips and a movie, enjoy your evening."

We screamed our lungs out, but to no avail. I'm not sure what Bobby told Mary, but I find it credible that she was not overly concerned about our whereabouts before she left. We spent the next six hours in that smelly little room, which we discovered by feeling about was indeed a closet but not the type that would hold an umbrella. As it turned out the little room was an abandoned *water closet* (toilet) that had been used by the mechanics working in the auto shop attached to Kitty's house. After seeing the state of the toilet after our internment, I was actually glad that we had spent the entire time in complete darkness.

After that, a truce was declared between Bobby and ourselves. We suspended our shenanigans and he promised not to lock us into any more closets. We actually joined Bobby and Mary out on the town for a night and they brought us to our first real casino to gamble as there was no real age of consent back then, at least none that anyone felt any compulsion to enforce. Many years later, I would return this hospitality when one of my younger cousins visited America and I took him out to his first strip joint and got him his first real lap dance. I felt it was the least I could do.

After that, Bobby and Mary spent a lot of time away from the house and that left us with our Aunt Kitty. That meant that we spent a lot of time driving around the streets of Dublin at all hours of the day and night as she could not, or would not, leave us at home alone while she went out on her taxi calls. We met a wide variety of interesting characters.

There was O' Toole, whose real name was Mr. Wheeler. All of Kitty's fares were phoned in to her from customers, oh, sorry "friends", who had heard about her through word of mouth, or a very discreet ad in the back of the Dundrum Church Bulletin. More often than not, those phone calls originated from the back of a pub, or in the case of O'Toole and others, the back alley of a pub.

Mary would often answer the phone and yell out "It's Mr. Wheeler", to which Kitty would respond "Good Lord O'Toole again? What sort of state is he in now?" and she would come over and take the phone and find out what sort of condition he was in and where he was, if he could indeed tell Kitty where he was. Often Kitty would have to play a game of twenty questions with Wheeler to figure out in which pub he was now legless. "Are you in Mulligans?...No, Davy Byrnes?...No, Sinnotts?...No, Deerpark Lounge?...No, Okay, describe what the bar looks like. There are two bars are there? Okay, close one eye and describe either one. Ugh huh, ugh huh, ugh huh, okay you're at The Goat. Stay there and we'll be by directly."

My aunt hang up the phone. "Damn that O'Toole. What a disgrace." I asked my aunt, "I thought that was Mr. Wheeler?" She said, "It was" "But you called him O'Toole" I pressed. She responded, "He certainly is, come on. We have to pick up Mr. Wheeler". I was confused. "But what about O'Toole? Is he with Mr. Wheeler?" "All too often" my aunt replied. I was getting that Abbott and Costello "Who's on First" feeling when I decided to drop it.

It was explained to me later that old Dubliners had a form of English Cockney Rhyming slang all their own. You see the London Cockneys (think My Fair Lady) had a form of slang where they substituted a word or phrase that rhymed for the word they intended. For example, if you said a girl had lovely "mince pies", you meant she had lovely eyes, or "trouble and strife" is slang for your "wife", "apples and pears" is slang for the "stairs", well you get it.

Well the old Dubliners did the same thing and if you said someone was "O'Toole", it meant he was "drunk as a rule" and that certainly applied to Mr. Wheeler, known more often as Mr. O'Toole, and that Summer we picked up many an O' Toole in the form of a Flannigan, Nolan, Maguire and more "O somethings" than on Overstocked Dot Com commercial.

Aunt Kitty hustled us into her taxi cab which at that time took the form of a Morris Minor. Morris was a car of English manufacture, and was sort of the Volkswagen Beatle of the British Isles. It wasn't terribly stylish, but it was rugged and dependable, with a large back seat making it ideally suited for Kitty's purpose.

Kitty approached the driving of her cab with much the same cavalier attitude she had toward the regulation of it. Speed limits were generally ignored or Kitty was ignorant of their existence, I'm not really sure which. Stop lights were given the respect they were due meaning the vehicle slowed to make sure there was no approaching cross traffic and then the Morris was gunned, the gears worked feverishly as the little motorcar exploded through the intersection hardly delaying its pressing mission.

On this occasion, we did indeed find Mr. Wheeler at the Goat, face down in a steak and kidney pie. My aunt threw a disgusted glance at the bartender who simply shrugged his shoulders, threw a bar towel over his shoulder and said as he turned away, "I'm sorry Kitty, but he said he was hungry." With the bartender's help, we loaded O'Toole into the Morris. My brother sat on one side of him and I sat on the other and together we formed two human bookends which served to keep the floppy Irishman upright. "Be quiet lads, maybe we can get him home before he wakes up", instructed my aunt.

It wasn't to be. Mr. Wheeler woke up and the mystery of the air sickness bags was solved. At one point in the journey, Kitty was forced to come to a particularly violent stop. The road must have been completely blocked, along with the sidewalk, to force Kitty to come to a complete halt. The sudden deceleration caused Mr. Wheeler to shoot forward hit the back of the front seat and then bounce back and land in pretty much the same position he started in, wedged between my brother and myself. "Augh, Jaysus Kitty are we home?", he moaned. My aunt replied with no attempt to hide her disgust, "No, we're not you old fool, now sit back and keep quiet". Wheeler replied, "I need a bag Kitty, where are the bags?" My aunt went from disgust to anger. "Oh no you don't, you drunken fool. I've just cleaned the seats back there. Don't you even think about it. Wait 'til you get home." Wheeler moaned. His head began moving in erratic orbits above his shoulders and he began making gestures with his hands as if he was trying to swat imaginary flies away from his face. My Aunt Kitty was looking at us through the rear view mirror. "Lads, he's going to blow. Quick grab a bag and hold it up for him."   My brother and I had no idea what she was talking about. We both looked at her and said, "Bags, what bags? What are you talking about?" My aunt was growing impatient. She knew disaster was moments away. "The bags you brought, the sick bags, they're in the seat pocket. Quick, grab one and give it to Mr. Wheeler". I looked around and there I saw, stuffed in a front seat pocket a handful of the air sickness bags we had taken from the plane. I quickly grabbed one and held it to Mr. Wheeler's face. He was obviously well versed in the drill as he grabbed the bag and quickly filled one up and then another with a soupy concoction of Guinness and steak and kidney pie. Well, at least the mystery of the sick bags was solved even if we did have to hold those vomit filled bags for another ten miles as we drove Mr. Wheeler home.

We had several more adventures with Mr. Wheeler during that summer and we picked up dozens of other "friends" of my Aunt Kitty's as she drove them all over county Dublin. We couldn't have spent five years in Dublin on our own and managed to see half the things we saw or have half the fun we had driving around the city in that old Morris Minor. We picked up characters both drunk and sober, but all of which had a unique character flaw or personal secret we heard exposed as Aunt Kitty gossiped with her various fares. But of all the clients of my Aunt, and of all the adventures we had in Dublin, our absolute favorite was Mr. Kipaliti.

Mr. Kipaliti was not Irish, and in fact he had no Irish roots at all. He was Italian in a country where immigration was almost nonexistent and emigration was the rule. In the early seventies he was an older gentleman, 60ish, who had come to Ireland after World War II to escape the desolation, hunger and hopelessness of his war ravaged homeland, hoping for a better life than what would be possible in his native Naples.

He may have chosen Ireland because in truth, the Irish were actually quite sympathetic with the Axis powers. After all, whatever you may think personally about Mr. Hitler or Mr. Mussolini, they were fighting the British and anybody who was killing Englishmen couldn't be all bad.

Although Ireland certainly missed much of the devastation of the war, it was hardly a bastion of economic opportunity. Before the war, Ireland struggled under thirty percent unemployment rates and after the war, Ireland stuck with tradition and continued to operate under crushing rates of unemployment, hitting and exceeding thirty percent per annum on a regular basis. The one good thing to be said about the Irish economy was that, unlike England, Ireland's factories and economic infrastructure had not been obliterated by the Nazi bombing raids as had England's great industrial cities and factories. Of course the reason for this was not that the Nazis had mercifully spared the Irish, or even thought of them as potential allies, it's because there was no need to wipe out Irelands industry or infrastructure as no great industrial cities or economic infrastructure existed. The only target of any value may have been the Irish agricultural production, but it hardly seems that it would have made a lot of strategic sense to launch massive bombing raids against herds of cows or try to obliterate the local sheep populace.

So Kipaliti ended up in Ireland, a young Italian out to seek his fortune. And seek his fortune he did. He ending up becoming quite a Horatio Alger story in his own right eventually owning several food processing plants, a dairy, an ice cream factory, a candy and crisp (potato chip) factory and several night clubs and restaurants around Dublin. My Aunt Kitty said he was a millionaire, the first one of those I'd ever met, and crazy as a loon. To Brian and myself he was terrific fun, a great fellow who attached himself to us in a sort of strange paternal way and treated us like his own two sons during that short, heady summer in Dublin.

Whether to just fit in,,   or simply because it's just so much fun, Mr. Kipaliti also took up the national pastime of his adopted country and began drinking to irresponsible excess. This of course was the reason he required so much of Aunt Kitty's services and in this regard, the man became more

Irish than the Irish themselves. I cannot honestly remember seeing the man sober, but in his defense, I only ever saw him at night.

When Aunt Kitty had a fare for her taxi service, it typically was either a regularly scheduled affair, such as bringing Mrs. McLaughlin to the market every Saturday morning, or it was phoned in on the only phone in the house. The nondescript black box hung on the wall in the front hallway, alongside the coat rack, a small chalkboard mounted next to it ever at the ready to record the details of the passenger to be retrieved.

Mr. Kipaliti was primarily a call in, and was always a night time fare. Whenever the phone would ring in the evening my brother and I would get very excited, hoping against hope that it was Kipaliti and we would be rescued from a dull evening staring at the fireplace to be off and about town ferrying Kipaliti to assorted pubs, nightclubs and restaurants until invariably Kipaliti would surrender to the cumulative effects of the Guinness, the whiskey and the hour and require that Aunt Kitty (and on more than one occasion Brian and myself) pour him into the backseat of the Morris and take him home.

The wonderful thing about Mr. Kipaliti, and the reason Kitty catered to his every need and gave preference over every other customer, scheduled or not, was that Kipaliti required that Aunt Kitty stay with him the entire night, with the meter running. He also was an almost uncomfortably embarrassing big tipper.

On the trips out with Kipaliti, we would join him at the pubs, nightclubs and restaurants, get our own table and have an open tab to whatever we wanted. In the restaurants that he owned, and they were several, Kipaliti would tell the manager, "Give the lads whatever they want. Let them enjoy themselves" and we would have essentially carte blanche in his establishments.

At one of the Kipaliti restaurants, a particularly upscale Italian supper club on Leeson St., my brother and I, in a Homeric display of American obnoxiousness, actually took over the piano bar, dismissing the extremely talented gentleman who was playing and started singing A Cappella Partridge Family songs to which we hardly knew the lyrics. We quickly emptied the more than full bar, but kept on singing as Kipaliti was in the back, completely legless, clapping enthusiastically and yelling "...give us another tune lads!"

It was taking Mr. Kipaliti back from a night on the town, that Aunt Kitty found herself engaged in what was probably one of the first slow speed chases I referred to earlier, which of course O.J. Simpson would later make so famous.

Now there are many European capitals that are famous for their horrendous traffic. Certainly London comes to mind, Paris and of course Rome, where it is almost a given that if you want to get from one side of the Eternal City to another, and do it in the same night, walking or stealing a scooter are probably your best options. The roads in Dublin, like all of these cities, were never meant for motorized traffic. The traffic arteries throughout the city originally started as footpaths, were upgraded for ox and cart and the last major improvements were to put some sort of a hard surface down to accommodate the high speed horse and buggies that were coming into vogue.

Mr. Kipaliti also hated the Dublin traffic, and I suppose that was yet another reason he did not drive anywhere. He also despised walking about town, as he never did seem to get used to the traffic in Dublin travelling on the opposite side of the road from his native Italy. I can tell you from my own experience of growing up in America and then spending several years in Ireland that it is very difficult to break the habit of instinctively looking left for oncoming traffic while crossing a road. Kipaliti had been hit twice while crossing roads in Dublin, and he was always an unusually nervous man in traffic.

Now in the early seventies the Dublin Town council had installed the newest craze in pedestrian safety when they put in marked crosswalks with pedestrian traffic signals at all the major and most minor intersections. Although we are all familiar now with these lighted "Walk/Don't Walk" symbols synchronized to the traffic lights and operated with a button by the pedestrians, at this time in Dublin, they were cutting edge technology. Mr. Kipaliti got in the habit of crossing roads only at intersections that had these new signs.

On one section of Leeson St., Mr. Kipaliti owned both a restaurant on one side of the street and a nightclub on the other. Although Kipaliti would have more than welcomed us, Brian and I were not allowed in the nightclub because of strict laws regarding minors in clubs after certain hours. Kipaliti took care of business at his night club and then crossed the street and took care of business at the restaurant, talking to managers, chefs, waiters and having drinks with more than a few of his patrons. He would then cross back over the road and go deal with the nightclub again. All the while we would sit at a table by a big window facing the street and eat all manner of fine Italian food, drink our fill of sodas and eat Italian desserts until we were ready to burst.

We would also watch through the window with great amusement as Mr. Kipaliti made his various trips across the street to the club. Now just because I said that Mr. Kipaliti would only cross the street at lights with a pedestrian crossing sign, doesn't mean that he successfully made the crossing. My brother and I would sit and watch laughing our heads off as Kipaliti would wait patiently at the light for the "Walk" sign to come on. When it did, he would cautiously still look both ways and then start slowly across the street. Perhaps the lights were designed with slightly faster pedestrians in mind, because invariably the light would change to "Don't Walk" while Kipaliti was still only half or maybe three quarters of the way across the street. Nevertheless, the changing of the signal would send Kipaliti into a panic and he would immediately reverse direction and scurry back to the original side of the street. This could go on for several changes of lights until Kipaliti either beat the clock to the other side, or Aunt Kitty would go out with a disgusted look on her face and help the old fellow complete his journey. Either way it provided us with great entertainment as we lapped up our fifth or sixth serving of Tiramisu.

It was taking Mr. Kipaliti home from one of his Leeson St. restaurants (the most congested part of inner city Dublin) that Aunt Kitty spotted an enforcement officer from the Dublin Taxi Licensing Bureau following her several cars back. (As it turned out later, several licensed Dublin cabbies had spotted Kitty shuttling around her fare and had contacted Enforcement) "Damn Paki Cabbies!" Kitty exclaimed, regardless of there being a complete lack of any proof as to the ethnicity of her accusers.

Now just a note here on inner city Dublin traffic. Although London, Roman and Parisian traffic may be more famous, Dublin has a unique angle to some of the problems of getting around a one thousand year old city in a motor car. The problem was that Ireland never really updated any of the laws regarding traffic in the city. As such, any person, and in Dublin it was more often than not a group of indigenous gypsies that the Irish call Knackers, could travel the roads of the city in horse drawn, ox drawn, goat drawn, sheep drawn or really any animal powered vehicle with impunity. As a matter of fact, they had to be given the right of way. The Knackers exploited this loophole in the law to good effect.

Frequently bands of these Knackers would flood into the city in their carts and carriages and park in front of shops, restaurants and pubs or block access to key side roads cutting off whole streets of pub owners and merchants to local traffic. Of course they were more than happy to move along and block off another section of town if the effected merchants would show their appreciation with a small donation. It was a great business for these Irish Gypsies. Between this business with the local merchants, their control of the Irish used auto parts market, and the fact that every one of them alive (and a few that weren't) were on the public dole, the Knackers did very well indeed. As a matter of fact when I was back in Ireland in the early nineties, there was a story of a marriage of a couple from two large Knacker families. An entire castle estate was rented for the week and the wedding parties arrived by helicopter. At the conclusion of the nuptials and a near riotous reception, the bride and groom left for their honeymoon on a private yacht.

Although it produced outrage across Ireland, nothing could be done and no one could prove that anything illegal had transpired. The entire transaction was paid for in cash, and being gypsies, nobody had any permanent addresses on record. As a matter of fact, to add a little insult to injury, a large group of the wedding goers apparently enjoyed the accommodations in and around the castle so much, they stayed behind for a couple of weeks camping in and around the grounds.

Local farmers began to complain as their sheep began to go missing and the smell of roasting lamb permeated the evening air. The local police finally got a court order for the removal of the Knackers, but still they did not leave. This time, they insisted, they wished they could leave, but they did not have petrol for their vehicles nor had the money to purchase petrol so that they could move along. Unbelievably, the local town in its desperation to be rid of these unwanted visitors actually purchased gasoline *and* delivered it to any and all Knackers declaring a need. They did finally move on, presumably to find their next mark.

Now as it turns out, Mr. Kipaliti knew a lot of these knackers, or more accurately, a lot of these Knackers knew Mr. Kipaliti. As I mentioned, Mr. Kipaliti was a very generous man especially when he was moved, if not by the Holy Spirit than certainly by spirits. I remember multiple occasions when we would be traveling down the road and he would shout out "Kitty, stop, stop" as if his leg had just caught on fire. He would then jump out of the cab and run over to a group of Knackers he had spotted and start handing out five pound notes until Kitty could come over and stop him, chastising him for wasting his money on such a lot.

Well as it turned out, the Knackers came to Kitty's rescue. As Kitty carefully maneuvered her unlicensed cab with its illegal passenger through traffic, trying to put as many car lengths as possible between herself and the gentleman from

189

the taxi authority, Kipaliti called out "Kitty, stop, stop.", but Aunt Kitty was not about to stop this time and give her pursuer the advantage. Not to be deterred, Kipaliti exited the cab despite Kitty's noncompliance and even though it was a slow speed chase as I mentioned, it was still impressive to see a man who had to be in his early sixties jump out of a moving cab, execute a perfect shoulder roll, and get to his feet unscathed.

Mr. Kipaliti ran over to a group of Knackers with a horse drawn flatbed cart and a horse drawn carriage, and started handing out five pound notes. His hands were gesturing wildly pointing to our car and then to the car from the taxi authority. My Aunt exclaimed "Oh BeJaysus not now!" but was then relieved to see Kipaliti running back to the car without her usual intervention. She was even more relieved when she saw the Knackers pull both of their carts directly into the traffic behind her car blocking her pursuer and one hundred other vehicles as well. Kipaliti just jumped back in the car and yelled "Go, Kitty Go!"

In the end, it was the drink that killed Mr. Kipaliti. But no, it's not what you think. What happened was that Mr. Kipaliti was trying to cross O'Connell St. one day, fighting his "Walk/Don't Walk" demons, when a Jameson's Irish Whiskey truck blew the red light and hit him straight on. He was pronounced dead at the scene.

FB Call Home

The summer passed quickly like a dream, and to my Aunt Kitty's delight and to our disappointment, the time was drawing nigh for our return to America. School was scheduled to start in about ten days and Brian and I were scheduled to report in to the sixth and seventh grades respectively, but we knew that something was definitely wrong.

We overheard a couple of anxious phone calls between my Aunt Kitty and my mother and from what we could gather there seemed to be some apprehension as to the whereabouts of Father Bueller. The spinsters apparently had returned some two weeks since. They claimed to have no current intelligence regarding the good father's whereabouts, having last seen him over a month earlier when he dropped them at their B and B one evening, bid them good evening, and disappeared without a trace. Neither my Mother nor Aunt Kitty had heard from Father Bueller since he had dropped us off at our aunt's with the parting remark "see you at the end of the summer."

This was a puzzling development for the spinsters but not catastrophic as they had their own tickets home. For Brian and I it posed a bit more of a problem as FB had our tickets and our fate was in his hands as far as returning to America went. As the start of school grew ever closer, the phone calls between my aunt and my mother become more numerous and more desperate.

Communication was certainly an issue. Of course in the early Seventies there were no cell phones, e-mails or text messages even in America, but in Ireland the advances in technology that were available at the time had not been widely embraced. Even what we call today "land line" telephones were hardly universal. Not all homes had a phone. The phone service in Ireland for years was run by the government, through a company called Telecom Eiren. Now even though we at the time had monopolies like Ma Bell running our phone system in America, this was a government monopoly with all the wonderful images that those two words conjure up. Even twenty years later when I moved to Dublin to live, I inquired as to getting a phone installed in my apartment. My rent was Eighty pounds a month and I was making about eight hundred pounds a month. Despite numerous reforms to the government monopoly, including partial privatization, the cost of phone installation in your home was three hundred and fifty pounds plus a three hundred pound deposit. This must be paid all up front and then you would be put on a list and could expect a phone in three to six months. I even asked "How will I know when you'll be out to install the phone?", and the response I got from the pseudo government employee was, "We'll ring you", and she hung up. I did without a phone even in the early nineties and needless to say, many did without back in the early Seventies as well.

However we did have the church, and my mother went to our pastor Monsignor Harkin to see if he could do something to help locate FB and at least get the tickets in our hands so we could get home. Fortunately, Monsignor Harkin had some personal contacts with the Vatican and an APB (All Papal Bulletin) was issued to be on the lookout for Father Bueller.

A newspaper story from County Galway showed some promise. The story described a distraught young couple who were planning to get married, showed up at the church with friends and family and then were no showed by the priest. However, as we dug into the story further, it turns out it was the father of the bride who had taken the priest who was to perform the wedding out drinking the night before leaving him two towns away in an attempt to sabotage the entire affair. No luck.

It was decided that the best place to look for Father Bueller would be in his home county of Clare. Besides his family, who had no idea where he was, that would be the place we would probably find the most people who may have heard from him recently. The first place we would start was with the Dempsey family. Father Bueller and his family knew the Dempsey family in County Clare and knew very well Mike and Rose Dempsey who had immigrated to Chicago. As a matter of fact, Father Bueller's first trip to America was not to Florida. He first went to Chicago. If anyone knew the whereabouts of Father Bueller it would be the Dempseys.

In Chicago, Father Bueller was the guest of Mike and Rose Dempsey for what turned out to be an extended stay. My family met the Dempsey's in the early Seventies as it was their custom to escape the harsh Chicago winters by renting a house on Clearwater Beach and attending church at St. Cecelia's during the three to four months of the worst winter weather up north. We spent every moment we could with the Dempseys when they were in Clearwater. It was a huge treat to actually have a house on the beach, and not just be down there for the day renting an umbrella and chairs by the hour.

We got to know the family very well. Two of the kids were the same age as Brian and myself and the oldest boy Mike, his father's namesake, was a great musician and singer of the Irish ballads. I learned many of the rebel songs I love to sing today sitting around that beach house at night while Mike played the accordion and sang songs like "Johnson's Motorcar", "The Man from Mullingar" and "The Twelve Drunken Nights".

Mike Dempsey was a larger than life figure and one of the many true Horatio Alger stories of which the Irish immigrants to America seemed to produce so many. He left his native county Clare in the early Fifties, about the same time my mother immigrated to New York. Mike landed in Chicago and, as the story goes, arrived on the scene with twelve dollars in his wallet and a pocket full of dreams.

His conveyance was a train from Grand Central to Union Station, disembarking at the latter, neither knowing anyone nor having anywhere to go. He ascended from the depths of the station to street level and began to walk along the west side of the Chicago River, when he came to a construction project currently arising along the river's bank.

The Tale, at the time that I heard it already had been elevated to the level of Sacred Lore amongst the Dempsey Family, was that Mike approached the foreman of the project and soon found himself operating a shovel, digging footers for the new building. Twenty years later, Mike Dempsey owned the seventh largest construction firm in Cook County and owned, at the time we knew him, somewhere on the order of four hundred apartments and a dozen or so additional office and industrial buildings in the Greater Chicago Area.

On a trip back to Ireland, Mike ran into Father Bueller. Clare not being a terribly big county, he knew of Father Bueller's family, and Mike's father knew Father Bueller's father and grandfather. They had a short friendly conversation over a pint at the local pub and as is the custom, or a general courtesy that carries about the same weight of sincerity as "how are you?", Mike, just prior to leaving the pub, said to Father Bueller as a parting remark, "If you're ever in Chicago, look me up".

Mike thought nothing more of it. Father Bueller started packing his bags. A month later, he showed up on Mike Dempsey's doorstep to cash in on his "invitation" to come visit.

I imagine Father Bueller was impressed. Mike had eight children and had a very comfortable ten bedroom house to keep them in. The house was actually designed by Frank Lloyd Wright and was located in the desirable North Shore area of Chicago. As a matter of fact, I know he was impressed because a month after his arrival, he was still there. Two months after his arrival he was still there. And three months after his arrival he had settled into a very comfortable routine of upper middle class American suburban life.

Father Bueller fit right into the affluent American neighborhood as well as the Dempsey household. Mike Dempsey kept a well- stocked bar, which Father Bueller put to good use. He also attended the local country club that Mike belonged to. He was not a frequent patron, only visiting with Mike on the infrequent occasions he had time for a round of golf or a drink at the Nineteenth hole.

He also did truly enjoy the Dempsey children and they, in truth, adored him. He attended the sporting events of the elder children, played with the middle kids and read at night to the younger ones. He also did not neglect his priestly duties. He said masses at the local church, visited the elderly in the area nursing homes and volunteered as hospital chaplain for the local parish. It truly was difficult to get too angry or upset with the good Father as he was truly a charitable person at heart and did strive to serve others.

However, as the months passed, Rose Dempsey, Mike's sweet but stern wife, insisted that something had to be done. Now you have to understand that to the Irish of this generation, priests were held in great esteem and also not a little fear. Priests had always been an authority figure and the Catholic Church was the final arbitrator of all issues in Irish life, including post Irish life. They decided factors like who went to Heaven, who went to Hell or who was condemned to dreaded Purgatory. One simply couldn't just come out and ask a priest to leave your house. Subtle hints about missing his homeland and compliments to the effect that he would make a great parish priest and shouldn't he think about taking a position somewhere fell on deaf ears.

Mike then had a stroke of genius. He decided that the best way to get Father Bueller to leave, was to make him *want* to go home. He bought Father Bueller a one way ticket back to Ireland and then began to hatch his plan.

On a day of his choosing, he called Father Bueller into the bar at the house, poured a couple of drinks and then gradually came around to the conversation he wanted to have. "Father, I can't tell you how grateful we are that you've come out to stay with us and it truly has been a blessing", Mike started out. Father Bueller though, didn't let him get very far, "Augh Jaysus Mike it's nothing at all. I'm glad to do it.", he continued. "Sure isn't it part of my calling to be of help to my fellow Christians?" But Mike knew who he was dealing with at this stage. He'd seen Father Bueller use his gift of the Blarney all over town to secure sports tickets, invitations to dinner and free drinks at bars across North Chicago. He wasn't about to fall victim to his rhetorical rapier, and grabbed back the reins of the conversation. "Augh, yes, indeed, and you've been nothing but a help to us. You've been like another parent to the kids and they adore you, and that's why I've been thinking about *your* parents back in Clare", Mike continued. "They're not getting any younger Father, and I know they must miss a son like yourself something desperate." Mike pressed the attack. "And what about your sister? You haven't seen her in an even longer time." Father Bueller parried, blunted Mike's verbal thrust, spun and thrusted back. "Augh, don't worry yourself about that." he said. "My brothers are with my folks and Fiona is busy with her husband and the 3 boys" Bueller replied, "As a matter of fact, now that we've had this conversation, I'm convinced more than ever, that this is where the Lord wants me to be"

Mike began to panic at this stage. He was losing control. If he wasn't careful, this silver tongued Irishman would end up having him completed tied in verbal knots and before he knew it he would end up as Father Bueller's legal guardian. Mike stammered losing his composure slightly as he struggled to regain the initiative. "Augh, Father, no, really, I think you need to be with your parents right now, I insist, I don't want to be held responsible for keeping you apart. Father Bueller though was having none of this talk and shot back. "Mike" he said in a more serious tone, "I know what you're trying to do. Quite frankly I'm really taken aback", he continued. "Why don't you just come out and say what's on your mind?"

Mike's face went blank. He was horrified. He'd tipped his hand and now he had insulted a priest. What horrible fate awaited him for this transgression? A trip straight to Hell? Thirty years of purgatory for his soul? His mind raced but he could think of nothing to say. He opened his mouth, but only air escaped. Finally he stuttered, "Father, look, ugh, honestly, I don't know what to say. It's just that with the kids and all, and Rose is, well, you know how Rose feels about you father, and like I said, the kids and all, we just all, as a family you know, all of us..." Bueller jumped in. "Mike, I'm really just very, very, very touched. You have no idea what this means to me." Mike's fear now went to confusion. His brow narrowed, his head tilted and he looked to Bueller for an answer to what the hell he was talking about. "I see what you're getting at Mike." he said. "You want me to bring my parents here to stay with us"

Dempsey nearly fell off his bar stool. He had been completely blindsided. While he thought he was masterfully executing his plan, his opponent had completely outfoxed him. During what Mike thought was a conventional rhetorical thrust and parry, Bueller had actually broken off the attack, feigning engagement, as he skillfully maneuvered around his opponent and delivered a near fatal blow from the rear. It was brilliant. Mike was clearly defeated, finished, and in his mind he was making plans to call in a subcontractor and redecorate a bedroom to Bueller's liking. It appeared he was going to be here for quite a while.

But as often happens, in our darkest hours is when we receive our greatest reprieve. As Mike sat at the bar dumbstruck now filling a water glass with Jameson's, Bueller rode in and provided absolution. "Mike, I can't accept your offer." he said. "But I do think you're right about my parents. I should go see them. But don't worry, I'll be back just as soon as I can." Dempsey couldn't believe his luck. Was this really happening? He shot back, "Oh no father. You take as long as you need. Your parents may have only a few years left. You should be with them during their final days, you must. And I'm going to buy you the ticket home."

And in the end, that's how Father Bueller left Chicago. However he had every intention of returning to Chi-town post haste. He did not realize that his ticket to Ireland was one way until he was at the airport boarding the plane.

Convinced that this must have been an oversight on Mike's part, once in Ireland, he contacted the travel agent to get the mistake corrected. Although the travel agent insisted there was no mistake, Bueller convinced her to change the ticket to round trip and charge Mike's credit card.

Mike was of course furious with the travel agent when he found out, but of course could not reverse course now without it looking like he did not want Father Bueller to return. It was then that he had a true stroke of genius.

As I mentioned, the Dempsey family spent their winters in Clearwater and attended St. Cecelia's during those winter months. They were also generous contributors to the church, a fact that did not go unnoticed among the clergy of the parish. Mike Dempsey decided to call in a favor.

He contacted Monsignor Harkin and told him the story of a wonderful priest he knew in county Clare that would be a wonderful asset to the parish and would be coming back to America in a couple of weeks. He encouraged Monsignor Harkin in the strongest terms that he should insist through the Bishop, that Father Bueller be assigned to St. Cecelia's.

Well, Father Bueller was notified that he had been assigned to St. Cecelia's parish, and would be part of the Missions. The return destination on his ticket was mysteriously changed to Tampa, and three months later ground was broken on a new parish hall next to the church.

My mother did manage to get a hold of Mike Dempsey. Unfortunately he had not heard from Father Bueller for several months so we were once again at square one.

Sweet Jaysus, Not the Jesuits!!

School had now started back in Clearwater and still no sign of Father Bueller. It was decided that regardless of where FB was, we should be back in school as well and my mother asked Aunt Kitty to enroll us in the nearby Jesuit Academy so that we would not get too far behind. The nuns at St. Cecelia's were tough. They were kittens compared to the Jesuits.

Americans were not very popular in Europe at this time. The Vietnam war was raging and television images of Americans killing indigenous peoples was on the air each evening. In addition, Nixon had just recently taken the US off the gold standard causing inflation to soar, and oil prices were going through the roof. Many were blaming America. The priest that would be our instructor at the academy was also blaming America, or more precisely, two Americans he just happened to have handy.

The Jesuit order or the Society of Jesus was founded by priests with a military background. They were known as God's Soldiers or God's Marines and father Patrick Michael certainly looked the part. He was six feet four if an inch and a solid 250. Years of rugby and Irish Hurling had cost him a few teeth but earned him a reputation for ferocity on and off the field. It took me only a few minutes to be wishing I was back in Sister Mary Wintergreen's class.

"Brady, Michael" *"Here sir"*, "Brady Patrick", *"Here sir"*, Clancy, Robert, *"here sir"* Durst, Kevin," *"here sir"*, Durst, Brian", *"here sir"*. "Brian and Kevin Durst. I believe you boys are both stranded here from America, is that right?" We nodded in confirmation. "Well now, shouldn't the cavalry be coming over the hill any minute to rescue you?" We said nothing. We could see where this was going. "Well Perhaps not", continued Father Michael, "the cavalry is probably busy in Vietnam bombing and killing innocents over there. I'm afraid you're on your own".

"Jaysus, it won't be too long before the two of you are given a tin hat and handed a gun and sent off to kill woman and children. You must be looking forward to that?" I couldn't help wondering what this guy's beef was, but he pressed the attack. "Well don't worry lads. There'll be plenty of time for you to kill your fellow man when you get back to America. "While you're in this class, you'll be learning about the love of Christ, the compassion of his one Holy and Apostolic Church and the goodwill of the Holy Roman Church towards all mankind."

I of course remained silent, but could not help thinking, "Well that should shorten our studies considerably as apparently we will not be touching on the First, Second, Third and Fourth Crusades, The Inquisition, the Medieval Witch Hunts, The slaughter of the Knights Templar, the burning of Joan of Arc at the stake, the burning of William Tyndale at the stake, the burning of Jan Hus at the stake, the burning of…., Hell, we could be out of here by lunch".

However, Father Michael continued. "Now class, not only is America burning babies in Vietnam, America's courts have said that it is okay to kill babies before they are born. I must admit that is a keen piece of Yankee ingenuity. It does make things more efficient. Mr. Durst, do you know how many babies you plan to kill in America this year? (I didn't know). You don't plan to kill any babies while you're here in Ireland do you Mr. Durst". (I didn't). He turned to a student in the front row. "Murphy, do we kill Babies in Ireland? (They did not) So Mr. Durst, just so you know, we will not tolerate any baby killing while you're in Ireland. Do you understand?" (I understood).

Now I'm not at all overly familiar with the curriculum at either Jesuit Seminaries or Catholic nunneries, but after suffering Sister Mary Wintergreen's Western Civ classes and now just

Father Michael's introduction to Jesuit education for the masses, I am sure that sarcasm was not just an elective, but part of the core curriculum at these Catholic institutions of higher learning. I'm sure courses for the future scholars and instructors these institutions churned out included: **Derision 101:** Pointing out your student's stupidity for all to see, **Mockery 201:** How to break the student's spirit through cruel references, **Scorn 202:** Let them know how much you really hate them. Yea, great stuff. The three "R's of Catholic education, Reading, 'Riting, and Ridicule.

But the Catholic Church believes in equality for all, and there was plenty of acerbity to go around. Father Pat quickly found another target. Misters Durst, you'll want to get to know Maguire over there." He turned and looked at a giant of a lad in the back row with a blank expression on his face. "Maguire, I understand you're off to America is that right?" Maguire nodded in the affirmative. Shaking his head Father Pat said, "Jaysus, that's incredible. You can't even find the schoolyard most days and you're off to America. Maybe Brian and Kevin can help you out when you get to America." Father Pat turned to look at us. "Now don't let that stupid expression on Maguire's face fool you. Oh he's an eejit all right, but he's thick enough to get the job done. You tell Maguire to dig a hole and he won't stop till he gets to China, isn't that right Maguire?" Maguire straightened up tall and erect in his seat and was beaming like a freshly praised puppy. Father Michael continued. "Not like the rest of you lot that don't know your elbows from your asses and all your smarty pants backtalk. Well the summer holidays are over as far as I'm concerned and we're going to knuckle down and get a small bit of work out of the lot of you."

Having to attend class every day took some of the charm off of life in Dublin. Being the personal whipping boys for a sadistic Jesuit priest with an exaggerated chip on his shoulder toward Americans didn't help either. Despite the efforts of Monsignor Harkin, The Vatican, the Irish Council of Bishops, the Irish National Police force and numerous local constabularies, there was still no sign of Father Bueller anywhere on the island.

Even August in Ireland can have its cold, damp days. It was on such a morning, stoking the old coal fired stove in my aunt's kitchen to create enough heat to make a cup of tea and fry an egg before heading off to see what form of abuse two hapless Americans would face at the hands of Father Michael, that our deliverance arrived.

The big brass knocker on my aunt's front door suddenly sang out announcing the arrival of an early morning visitor. Kitty answered the call opening the massive red door to find Father Michal Bueller standing on the threshold looking a good thirty pounds heavier since the start of the summer, but still retaining the same mischievous grin he had when we last saw him drive out of sight in June.

"How"ya Kitty? Jaysus, you're looking grand. Are the lads ready to go? We've got a flight to catch at 7. Is there time for a cup of tea?"

Gobsmacked would not adequately describe my aunt's reaction to seeing Bueller in the doorway. She stammered and stuttered trying to first ask Father Bueller where he'd been and then explaining to him what they had been going through trying to find him. "Augh Kitty, it's been an absolutely desperate situation all around. I must tell you about it sometime over a cupa " He glanced at his watch. "But no time for that now. Lads grab your bags we've got to go." Kitty must have had a million unanswered questions and I'm sure a few choice words for the padre, but she also recognized that she had this one last shot to get us home and it wasn't to be missed.

My aunt hustled us upstairs and all our belongings were unceremoniously stuffed into the bags with which we arrived. My aunt assured us, "I'll post to you anything left behind, now hurry and get downstairs before he leaves."

When we got back downstairs -' Bueller was already outside in the car, gunning the engine and leaning on the horn. "Let's go lads or you'll make us miss our flight."

It would be 15 years before I saw my Aunt Kitty again.

We made our flight and crossed back over the Atlantic, our carry-on bags again much heavier getting on the plane than getting in the car. The trip was uneventful. We had our lower floor seats while FB passed the flight comfortably ensconced upstairs. I can only imagine that Aunt Kitty called Mom because she was there at the airport waiting for us. After a brief meeting with my mother, Father Bueller decided, even though we were essentially going to the same place, to take a taxi home by himself.

Mom and Father Bueller of course eventually made up and she even became a sort of De Facto Church secretary for him when he was given his own parish in Lutz, just north of Tampa. I learned later that this was hardly a promotion for him as the "Parish" was a temporary metal structure, the rectory an old donated mobile home and he had the charge of less than forty five souls.

I think Monsignor Harkin, who was being shortlisted for the next bishop, decided that FB was just too high maintenance and sent him to the boonies where he hoped he could be of little trouble. That hope was dashed when Monsignor Harkin got a call early one morning from the Pasco County sheriff's office that they had Father Bueller in custody for driving his riding lawnmower to the Handy Mart for more beer. Apparently the padre was confused and didn't understand what the problem was claiming it was the only responsible thing to do because he was too drunk to drive.

As the years went on we saw Father Bueller less and less. My mother stayed in touch with his sister in Dublin and we found out that he was given an early retirement and went to live at an old priest's home in his native Clare.

He went to his final reward not quietly but with a bang, literally. After returning to the home one night after an evening with comrades at the local pub, he discovered that he had been locked out of the home. Unfortunately FB had been assigned a second floor room. Not wanting to wake anyone he decided, at sixty eight years old, to climb up the drainpipe to bed. Almost to the top, the drainpipe detached from the wall along with Father Bueller. He plunged the two stories to a concrete drive and unfortunately never recovered from his injuries.

We continued growing up in Clearwater. And Clearwater continued to grow up. My hometown went from a quiet winter snowbird destination to become part of "Tampa Bay" an area encompassing some three million people. They say you can never go home, and it is true.

We left St. Cecelia and went to Clearwater High and Central Catholic, off to college, on to careers, family and kids of our own. Many more summers came and went from that one we spent in Dublin courtesy of Father Bueller's addiction. Each had their attractions, summer flings with the fairer sex, camping trips to the mountains, learning to drive, college road trips and even a trip to Italy. Those summers of my boyhood, the fights, the forts and the friends made me who I am today. However, that one summer in Dublin will always stand out as an adventure that never could have been planned and one that could have only been made possible by an incredible character like Father Bueller.

Made in the USA
San Bernardino, CA
18 April 2017